Mind Synergy

Bev Baker

New Generation Publishing

Acknowledgements

My Teachers

When I decided to stop singing for a living, I had no clue as to what I wanted to do. My sister Eve said I was "unemployable" and to a certain extent she was right. I had no qualifications to speak of and no real interest in anything. One day she invited me to a weekend course, I think someone had dropped out. I tried to get out of it but she wouldn't take no for an answer. At that weekend I was introduced to the world of psychology and, in particular, psychotherapy. It was a world that I didn't know existed and I was hooked. Psychology was my entry point to realising that I had a brain, and a very good one at that. I acknowledge Eric Berne, Eve Baker and all psychologists out there who awakened my passion for learning. I also salute Albert Einstein. When I was younger I used to be afraid of him. Physics wasn't my thing and my science teacher made sure that it stayed that way. I thought that people who studied science were strange. I have come to see that science is great. I particularly acknowledge Einstein because he was so brilliant and at the same time, playful. Who can resist a playful genius?

All the quotes in this book are his.

Dedications

To my Mother

What a woman!

My sister and I were well-known for our parties when we were teenagers. Where other parents would never allow it my mother was all for it. Many years later we realised that she used to stash the drinks left over for her own use. There was a guy in our year known as the hard guy. No one messed with him. I invited him to our parties; it was either that or get beaten up. Can you imagine my astonishment when I woke up the next day after one of our parties to find the guy, who should remain nameless, cleaning the kitchen! My mother had tamed the bad boy. They chatted, she told stories, she made him laugh. She taught me about connecting with people.

To my Chino

When we first met, he possessed about five words of English and I had slightly more of Spanish. When we decided to be together we knew the road would be hard. It was and it still is. Who knew that a Zen-like dancer from the outskirts of Havana would teach me so much about me? One of the wisest decisions I have ever made is deciding to get him to ask me to be his wife.

To my Jack

Jack is my son. I remember one time we were having our usual discussion. I was trying to relay my latest theory, as is my wont, and he was telling me in no uncertain terms why it wasn't a theory. Suddenly I stopped in mid-sentence and just looked at him. In front of me was this super intelligent guy who wasn't taking any nonsense from me just because I had the honour of being his mother. I knew in that moment I had done my job. I feel proud to know that I have had some part in raising such a beautiful human being.

To my Students

Every time I start a class or take on a client, I get a little apprehensive. For about 30 seconds I forget everything I know. Blank. It is then that I turn to God and ask for help. It always comes...when I step into 'doing my thing', and I need no theories, models or slide show. I demand a lot from my students. No mobiles, no computers or lazy thinking. I need ears, imagination and total participation. When you have been trained by me consider yourself trained because it is my intention never to teach you anything that doesn't already exist within. My job is to bring it out. I don't teach stuff... I teach people. My students are my inspiration. They have taught me everything I know.

CONTENTS

~Part One~

"Everything should be made as simple as possible, but not simpler."

~Chapter One~

Let's Get Started!

Hi there and welcome to my master class.

My name is Bev Baker, international trainer; that is true. Motivational speaker, and communications expert; so, I am told. I am married with one son and live in London's fair city.

It is my students and clients who have encouraged me over the years to write. It is a genre to which I am unfamiliar. So here goes…

I wanted the book to be heavyweight, something that could change the thinking of mankind. Something that would make me go down in history. No pressure, then!

If I couldn't have that, at least I should make the book club on Oprah. I imagined selling millions of books, like 'Fifty Shades of Grey'. I was going to be the next writing sensation. It's easy, right, all you have to do is visualise what you want and puff… let it go. I did that. I wrote a 'mood board', don't ask! To create a 'mood board' you write down all the things you want and all that that thing means to you. I did that! I went for long walks, as is my wont, and I would virtually write the book in my head out there on the streets.

When I returned from my walks and tried to put pen to paper, fingers to keyboard, and mouth to Dictaphone nothing happened. Nothing! Nada! Absolutely zilch! I studied hard. I surrounded myself with knowledge. I thought that if I overdosed on knowledge then surely it would flow on to the page. No! I read somewhere that Wayne Dwyer, the self-help writer and motivational speaker, when writing a book, would put all the books of his gurus around him to create a sacred space. All the energy and genius from his guides would then seep into his being and fill the pages. He reports that he could write for days uninterrupted and without the need for food or sleep. I tried it. I surrounded myself with the works of Gandhi and the Buddha. Nothing!

I found myself breaking away from my blank page with an overwhelming need for ice cream, to check the washing as it spun around in the washing machine or check Facebook. I 'liked' everything in sight. I remember one day when I was supposed to write up an important piece, I had an overwhelming desire to call my sister and talk to her on the telephone for three hours. By the time I had finished my conversation it was way too late to start writing. Funny, that! Spring became summer and summer became a distraction. I read quantum and mechanical physics. I studied various religions. I invented models and quite impressive questionnaires. None of this yielded more than a few pages. I was bored with myself.

The worst thing that I ever did was telling people about my plan, and my advice to you is if you want to achieve something, never do this. Don't tell anyone what you are doing until it is well underway and there is so much momentum you cannot be stopped and they can't put you off your stroke. Actors are well-known for not talking about upcoming projects. They believe that by talking about them they put a curse on it and it will never happen. I know it is plain superstition, but why risk it? Nonetheless, I thought it was a good idea to announce to my family, friends and students for the umpteenth time that I was writing a book. I thought by declaring my ambition I would be held to it. Most friends and family said, "That's nice, dear". They had heard this declaration many times before.

There goes Bev with one of her "I need to get the message to the world" ideas again.

But my students, they were not the same as my friends and family. They wanted the book, they willed the book.

They sent me ideas. They asked me how the book was getting on. The short answer was that it wasn't getting on anything but my nerves. The book was driving me crazy. I was starting to hallucinate. I can report now that one night I actually had a dream that the book had been written and had received amazing reviews. I was the toast of the town. Imagine my dismay when I woke up to find that not only was I not the toast of the town, but the book was nowhere to be seen. That dream swung me into depression for a week!

I decided that I didn't want to write anything. I had nothing to say. Obviously everything in this genre had been said by more eloquent scholars than me. Who was I kidding? So I paused. I took a beat. Days became months.

One day I was listening to Oprah. If anyone has the answer then it's Oprah. On her program that night was an interview with Pharrell Williams. He is the guy that wrote and sung the hit song 'Happy'. This song has become a phenomenon in so far as it was number one for most of 2013 and 2014 in numerous countries. If you go to YouTube you see so many millions of entries for that song it is crazy. People did their own video to it and sent it in. Countries did their own version of it, from Africa to Alaska. Teams did versions of it for their companies' team building. That song went viral. The song was one of those songs that come along from time to time, and it just did it for a lot of people.

The thing that got me about the interview was how humble the man Pharrell was. He spoke simply and yet I was in no doubt who the man was. He said that for so long he had tried to be something he was not. He had tried to be 'that guy', like, Jay-Z or Kanye West. He said that he realised that trying to be someone he was not, would mean that he would always come in at second place. That guy was that guy.

He said that he decided to be himself and try to be number one doing that. He also said something that was profound for me and woke me up. He had been asked to write the title track for *Despicable Me 2*. He wrote and wrote nothing. He thought, "How do great song writers write the song?" Nothing worked and nothing came. He then, after nine attempts, decided that he could not write a masterpiece trying to emulate someone else. It was the same as second guessing them. And why would his song be of any significance? It would only be a cheap reproduction of some other song. When he realised that he had to be himself and he had to do him, then the masterpiece came. That's how the song 'Happy' was born. It was my epiphany!

I emptied my mind of all preconceived ideas and plans of going on Oprah. I sat down and wrote the book I am proud to write.

One theory took me to another, yet I found that the more books I read the more confused I became. First, many of the theories are contradictory. Second, the style of writing left me cold. I have always found that the best approach to anything is to keep it simple.

What I am about to put across will read in parts like science fiction.

If it causes you to think about yourself then I am happy. If my words cause you to do your own investigation, I am happy. If you find that you don't like what you are reading, that's also fine. Come up with your own theory and write your own book. There is room for many points of view. Just because you disagree with me doesn't make me wrong. Just because you agree doesn't make me right. I am not relying on conspiracy theories either. This would mean that there was some sort of superpower pulling strings that you don't know about. I think that these so-called superpowers simply have found out how things work and you don't.

I have a point of view and I want to talk to you about it. My subject is you. This book, or whatever it turns out to be, is intended to give you food for thought and change the way you see yourself. Nothing will be the same again. Believe me. There will be a blip in your reality. There will be loads of questions, exercises and activities for you to do. This book will run just as I run my training classes. In other words, I write exactly as I speak. What you see is what you get! I am not precious; I don't particularly care if you throw this book against the wall. Strong reactions are most welcome!

This book is between me and you. I have poured everything I have into these pages. I don't really care if this book never makes it onto a bestsellers' list or on to Amazon. I have to write this book. Why? Because I said so... And my word is law in my world; world that sits between my ears and behind my eyes, that is. If I didn't write this book I could never tell my students to "go for their dreams" ever again. I would be a charlatan. I don't want to contribute to the world in that way.

How to get the most out of this book

I am writing this book in the same way that I deliver a class. You can read this book as you will. You can read it straight through or dip into it from time to time, allowing the ideas to sink in. I myself would prefer it if you read it and did the exercises as you went along, as the concepts will be fresh in your mind and your mind will already have assimilated them. I have written this book in this format because I am frustrated with books telling me I need this or that but giving no real clues how to achieve it. You need to improve your confidence or de-stress they say, then they spend a considerable amount of time talking around the subject but they fail, in my opinion, to deliver the goods. I want them to tell me what to do. If you do this or that you will see an improvement. It may be just me but I like things spelt out for me.

I am making my claim here. I am going to tell you how to get confidence or whatever you want, just as I have for thousands of my students and clients. Step by step. I wouldn't be much of a trainer if I set objectives and by the end of the class my students had nothing but a few quotes and examples. When my students come out of a class with me they know they have had training!

Your time is valuable and I know that if you are going to sit down and read this book you want results. Tangible results! Also I know how adults learn, and usually they want something in a format that works, when they want it! Not, this may be useful somehow, but you have to figure it out!

What does the title *Mind Synergy* mean anyway?

Your mind is the element of you that enables you to be aware of the world and your experiences. It is where you live, or it is where you should live, in your head. Have you ever questioned your thoughts? Have you ever stopped to analyse why you think the way you do and whether the thoughts and feelings you have are good for you or do they cause you to worry and suffer? Where do your thoughts and feelings come from anyway?

Consider these comments:
"I am in two minds…"
"I gave him a piece of my mind…"
"I can't take my mind off it…"
"I'm keeping my mind busy…"
"I have a mind to go there…"

You have probably used one or more of these phrases before. In each phrase there is a subject pronoun, which is the 'I' you refer to when you are speaking about yourself, and the object, which is your mind. Your mind is therefore something you possess and use. The question here is, are you using it to good effect? Who is in charge, you or your mind? Who is leading the show?

If you give someone a piece of your mind or you want to get something off your mind, what is left? Is the mind something that is always renewing itself or is it static? Is the mind just one entity or do you have many minds? All in all, it seems to me that there is more to the mind than meets the eye.

'Synergy' is the word used when two or more organisations or substances are brought together to produce an effect greater or different than the sum of its separate parts. You may have heard the phrases:

'Two heads are better than one'
Or
'Many hands make light work'.

Those phrases describe synergy. You may have come across synergy at work; the usual description is that 'the sum of the whole is more than the sum of the individual parts'. Synergy calls for interaction and working together. Synergy happens in nature, in science and in humans.

If you pick something up with one hand, you would think that if you used your two hands you would have twice as much power. Wrong! If you use two hands you will have twice as much power and then some. A perfect way to look at synergy in action is through music. All the parts of an orchestra are great in their own right but when you put them together, it is beautiful. Another example is a chef; s/he knows how to put one element with another in order to get the most out of each and to create a meal fit for a queen. Mathematically speaking $2+2=4$, but with synergy $2+2$ can $= 5$ or 10 or 105, or whatever you want it to be. Who knows what can be achieved when components, compounds and elements interact? They spark each other or they bring out something in each other. Synergy is like magic!

Now imagine if you could have your mind working in

perfect harmony for you. What would you be able to achieve? Or to put it another way, what would you not be able to achieve? Mind synergy is when you have all the parts of your mind working together to support you so that you can live the life of your dreams.

And how do I know that the contents of this book works?

How can I state categorically that this book will change your life? Because of the Law of Correspondence. This law is universal and you can apply it to everything. It applies to absolutely everything, whether you know it or not. It states that 'as above, so below' and everything has its own corresponding counterpart. 'As inside, so outside'. There can be no other way. The universe is made this way. There is harmony and agreement between everything that exists under the heavens. If you understand the electron, you understand the stars. If you understand the stars, you understand the electron. Everything is a mirror of everything else and everything is energy. You may think that there are different energies but there isn't, it's all one energy operating at different frequencies. If you look into your mind you will understand why and how things happen or don't happen in your life. If you look into your life you will see how your mind works. If you lack confidence in your life it is because you have a set of beliefs in your mind that actually support having a lack of confidence. There is a phrase that I remember as a student which sums up the law of correspondence in a nutshell, it is this: rubbish in, rubbish out!

The object of this book

The object of this book is to change the energy frequency in your mind. To dissolve thought systems that do not support you and to release trapped energy that will allow you to realise your every wish.

By the end of this book, and by completing the exercises therein, you will have the self-esteem, confidence, guts and the drive to live your life just as you want it to be. The change occurs internally so that you can have maximum impact in your life.

I have designed these exercises with 21 years of experience in the field of therapy, all corners of psychology, physics, Buddhism, my personal observations and other disciplines too numerous to mention. It is a cocktail of what works. There are 40 of them in total. They may appear simple and that's fine because there are no excuses for you not to do them. There are exercises and activities which are 'one offs' and there are those you will learn as you did your mobile number. All of them are easy-peasy!

The idea is for you to follow the mind synergy exercise program for 21 days. Twenty-one days is the number of days, purported by some psychologists, as necessary to break a habit. I don't know if that is right or wrong. It seems like a good number to start with. Three days is too short and 321 days is way too long. While they debate whether it is 21 days or 66 days, let's crack on. I think that 21 days are a number of days which are manageable.

It also depends on your starting point of course. The exercises can be repeated over and over again if need be. You can do 21 days on, 21 days off, and then 21 days on until you feel you are where you want to be. If you need to do the 21 days again, then simply repeat the exercises which are significant for you. If you need more self-esteem you will be drawn to those exercises, and so on!

A little advice...

It is best for you to choose a time to follow the program when you have time to devote to yourself. Don't choose the moment when you are stressed out and overworked.

You have to give yourself a chance at success. If you miss a day, no big deal, just pick up where you left off. If you miss more than three days, I suggest you start again. The purpose of the exercises is to clear your mind of old archaic beliefs and habits that are limited and limiting. You have to form new habits. I don't know how old you are, but you've had your patterns of thinking all your life. They will not give up without a struggle. You may find that you feel a little out of kilter for a few days. It's just the same as if you said to yourself, "Every morning from now on I am going to take the stairs at work instead of taking the lift." The first couple of days may be novel. You may even feel self-righteous as you watch your co-workers take the lift. Come day five or six your body has lost its sense of humour and it will scream at you. "Take the elevator!" This is the time when most people give up and give in. Continue.

If you get over the first week or so, the exercises will become part of your daily routine and by week three they will be second nature.

You can conduct these exercises anywhere and anytime. They are exercises you conduct by yourself and with yourself. You do not need anyone else. This is an inside job.

I recommend that you do the exercises at least twice a day. The best time is first thing in the morning when your mind is nice and fresh. Or at least it should be! And last thing at night when your mind is too tired to argue with you. If you fall asleep while doing the exercises that is perfectly fine. However, if you are waiting in line at the bank... do the exercises! If you have a moment to kill while you wait to be put through on the telephone...do the exercises. If you are preparing dinner...do the exercises.

There is no secret to the exercises. You can second guess what is going on if you want, but that is not the object of the exercise. I have devised these exercises after 21 years in the business of training people to be amazing. I have condensed all my work into 21 days of self- study for you. I think it is a good deal; 21 years for 21 days!

Lastly, I recommend you do the exercises as they come up for maximum results.

Around days 7–12 you will start to have more energy and feel more positive.

Days 13–18: You have more clarity of thinking, more focus and concentration and clearer communication.

Days 18–20: Feeling good about yourself; higher self-esteem; greater confidence; better sleeping and fitness; more decisive.

Day 21: Your wonderful creative self will show up. And you will be laughing!

I reckon that each exercise should take you about ten minutes a day.

So, what is your goal?

Write down what it is you want to achieve.

On a scale of one to ten how proficient are you right now (one is very low, ten is high)?

How will you know you have succeeded?

Example:

I want to be confident. My confidence level right now is 3 out of 10. I will know I have succeeded when I can deliver a presentation to my colleagues without panic.

I am not going to quote lots of authorities, I find it unnecessary and it will break up the flow (if there is one) of my thoughts. It is very difficult to set the tone for this book. I didn't want it to be an academic text, you know the ones with complicated drawn out theories that make you want to groan. Neither did I want something light and fluffy, only suitable for a book bin in a supermarket.

That is my promise. Read on…And you will see that I keep my promises!

So let's go… Let's write a book… Let's see what unfolds!

"Everything is energy and that's all there is to it."

~Chapter Two~

What's Going On?

Let's begin by asking a question.

"Who are you?" Yes, you heard me. "Who are you or who do you think you are?"

How do you describe the walking talking phenomenon that is you?

Jot down a few words as they occur to you. Write your responses in the margin of this book.

Have you got something? How easy or hard was it to answer this question?

Have you answered it by defining your personality traits? For example, if you say you are friendly, I should agree, right? It's a nice enough trait to have.

Is there more to you than that?

Of course there is.

So I repeat...

"Who are you?"

Let's pause a minute whilst you go through the types of answers you may have considered.

Let's start with your name. Are you your name?

Those arrangements of a few letters of the alphabet, is that you?

Long, short, hyphenated or double barrelled, easy to pronounce or very difficult, is that who you think you are?

I would suggest that there is plenty more...

Do you feel as if you should know or that you know but you just can't find the words to express yourself? Or is it the case that you have no clue?

God knows what your parents were thinking when they named you. What and who did they want you to turn out like? Which film star was your mother secretly in love with when thinking about naming you? When you were born perhaps your facial expressions sealed your fate. Did you look like a 'Charles' or more of a 'Kylie'? My nephew made a yelping sound when he was born and that was it, his fate was sealed. He became Michael, after Michael Jackson.

Were you named after a mystic like Mohammed or a character from history like Alfred the Great, who has significance in your country? Was your father making a political statement with your name?

You may not be aware but your name holds your parents' hope for the future. When you were born and as they held you in their arms, along with the naming ceremony was the hope that you would bring honour and respect to the name. There was so much riding on you; perhaps you would be the first to go to university. Perhaps you would be the first to leave the one horse town and make it in the capital.

"Oh where is your son, George?" they'd ask.

"He's away slaying dragons," your mother replied with pride.

What would happen if you decided to change your name? Many have done it. Many have had it changed for them.

I remember an Indian guy whose name was made up of only consonants, it seemed. The name was too time-consuming for the machine operatives in the factory in which he worked so they changed it, just like that. They decided to call him 'Sid'. Two thousand years of tradition and heritage lost just like that. What's in a name...right!

So instead of being Bev ... I became Vanessa! I love that name! I should have been a Vanessa. It sounds sophisticated and exotic. In Cuba, my husband's homeland, they cannot get their tongues around the 'v' in my name so instead of calling me 'Bev', they call me 'Beff' or 'Beef', very sophisticated! My mother named me after Beverly Hills, which she thought was a good idea. She would hold court when I was young, explaining to people that my name meant 'hill'.

16

It doesn't.

So my name is the name of a hill and a very famous one at that, but it doesn't mean 'hill'.

Anyhow, back to what I was saying…If I decided to be Vanessa, would my life experience be any different? Would my parents and teachers treat me any differently?

Being called Vanessa wouldn't solve my problems. Lord knows what my Latin in-laws would make of that name.

All in all, when you look at it, your name is a shortcut way of addressing you and getting your attention.

Can you image life without names?

"Where is that man?"

"Which man?"

"The one who has red hair and is married to that woman."

"Which woman is that?"

"The one that is blonde with blue eyes."

"Do they have any children?"

"Yes they have children… they have twins."

"Oh yeah! I know them… they are not in."

"Please could you tell him that his mother called!"

Nightmare!

I once had a class where there were five Alex's in the class. Every time I directed a question to one of them, five heads bobbed up at me. So I had the task of finding distinguishing features about them so that I could single them out. They were not their names. They had completely different experiences in life and had drawn different conclusions from those experiences.

One time I was talking to this guy and he asked me my name.

"Beverly," I said. I hadn't learnt to shorten it yet.

"You look like a Beverly," he said.

"What does a Beverly look like?" What a dumb thing to say!

"Very naughty," he smirked, "I had a Beverly as a girlfriend once and she was very naughty."

Needless to say, like an investigative journalist on a Sunday newspaper, I made my excuses and left. I was not going to spend my time with a guy who told me I looked like my name and was hoping that I had the same characteristics as an ex-girlfriend. Saints preserve us!

Have you noticed how many people individualise their names, trying so hard to be different? Jeffrey becomes Geoffrey. Steven is Stephen. Change a letter or add a letter and stand out from the crowd.

So you are not your name. There is more.

What about the job you do... is that a reasonable way to define you? Not even close.

Again, if you were to change jobs tomorrow and decided to test chocolate ashtrays for a living, you would still be you. A little crazy perhaps, but in essence you would still be you.

Your job is what you do, it is not who you are.

Make a list here in the margin of all the jobs you could do right now!

Me, I could be a dance teacher or a reasonable chef...I could be a therapist again. Now, I am a writer!

So let's see... you are not your name and nor are you your profession!

What about your roles in life? You are a son, a daughter, a wife, a brother, a friend, a neighbour... Ah, the list goes on and on...

Each of these roles requires you to act a part!

Yes, act! You are certainly not the same person when talking to your mother as you are when talking to your lover. Nor are you the same person when talking to the boss as you are when talking to a very close friend. Each of these roles carries with them certain expectations and codes of conduct. They are part of you, yes, but not wholly you.

Some of the roles that you act out every day may

18

actually be in conflict with each other. Being a model anything or anyone is hard work.

Enough of trying to decipher who you are, I will come back to that in a while.

I want to spend a moment talking about my approach to this book. It nearly didn't happen.

Scientists have been humming and hawing about some pretty big questions for centuries. The Bible informs us that God made the earth in six days and on the seventh day he rested. It is a lot to take in... I agree! Hard core physics could never accept this concept. It was not mathematical and furthermore, it was too much like a fairy tale. Scientists came up with Big Bang theories and string theories that no one understood or really cared about. The problem with it all is that scientists can only deal with what they see or what they can reproduce time and time and again. So, in other words, if you cannot prove it, it doesn't exist.

One of the things I do not get with science is why it is so defensive. History is littered with inventors, artists and people who thought differently and who died in a pauper's grave just because the so called guardians of knowledge didn't agree with them.

Great thinkers of the day are the same great thinkers who said the world was flat and that air consisted of only phlogiston.

I remember one time and let me tell you the last time... I was lecturing in a major teaching hospital in the centre of London. I was to teach a group of psychiatrists, psychologists and the like the latest idea of the moment which was Neuro Linguistic Programming. Oh my lord! I felt as if I had committed some evil crime against humanity. Had I tortured kittens or told a child that there was no Santa? No! For my sins all I had put in front of them was an idea. A concept! No, it would not see them out of business. Neither would it invalidate the book they were writing or the consultancy position they had secured.

Actually, the intention was to enhance them. I left that day with one thought in my head and that thought is unprintable. I would need a psychiatrist if I was going to ask any of those pompous gits for advice. Hey scientist, why so defensive? Why so intimidated by new thinking?

I would have thought that the object of science is to find things out, to explore knowledge, but not just knowledge for knowledge's sake, otherwise what is the point? If you are going to apply knowledge, you are going to have to brush up on other disciplines. The object of the exercise is not to poo-poo other ideas as rubbish, rather to see how and if other disciplines can teach you anything more about your own discipline. Science has shot itself in the foot by claiming itself to be superior to every other font of knowledge, so it cannot actually go any further. Science is about how things interact and relate to each other. Because science has 'crowned' itself as the king of knowledge it can only interact with itself. I wonder how many people with great ideas are put off by the pomposity of science. I wonder how many not so persistent or resilient people go to their grave along with the 'big idea'.

I say to my students, "I don't care what your discipline, just don't be an elitist. You will make yourself obsolete. If you are an engineer, pick up a book on cooking. There is a science to it. If you are a shop assistant, pick up a book on quantum mechanics. You will see that there is an art to it."

I was teaching a class of engineers in Moscow, all of whom had a science background and quite a few had PhDs. The funny thing about it was that although they could explain their theories to me, they could not explain what those theories meant for me in my life. How does physics explain emotion if you are an emotional person? Or is that one of those 'by design' oddities of being human? During my class one of the guys lamented that he wouldn't find a girlfriend. I teased him.

Why can't you use quantum physics to find yourself a partner? How does quantum physics explain the fact that there are people all over the world who are lonely, stressed and depressed?

What scientists seem to agree on is the importance of energy. In fact everything is energy. Therefore energy is all that is. Everything is about the energy you put into something. Stands to reason if you study hard you will get something out of it. Yet there is more to it than that. It is all about understanding energy. Especially the energy which is you. It about understanding the composition of energy, the nature of energy and most importantly, what happens when energy is blocked.

I don't know about you but sometimes it takes the willpower of Hercules to write a paper or tidy the house. I don't have the same problem when it comes to eating ice cream somehow. There is an energy force inside you informing your actions. Do this... do that! These are your thoughts and feelings.

OK, next question, what is the composition of energy? Scientists on this path inform us that energy is made up of particles and waves. So particles are the energies that you may see and waves are the energies that you know are there yet you can't see them. Take air for example, air is made up of waves because it moves and yet stays the same. Air is also made up of particles that can be transformed into matter such as nitrogen.

The double slit experiment turned everything on its head. One of my lovely students, Ioan Cosmin Radu, brought this experiment to my attention. By this time everyone knew I was struggling with the concept of the book. I wasn't winning.

Back to the double slit experiment. Up until this experiment scientists were pretty confident that light was made up of particles.

An experiment was set up to pass light particles known as photons one by one through two slits in a screen to see how they would format on the wall behind them. Normally, if you did this without the slits or passing them one by one, the light would just flow into the space. This is what happens when you turn on the light at home. So the photons were passed through the slits one by one. This is what happened. It was as if the photons had some sort of intelligence. *They* decided which slit to go through and more than that *they* also decided by some cosmic force to become waves.

The key word here is that the photon 'chose'!

This was big for the scientists. They decided to construct a camera to determine just when the photons became waves. What was that crucial tipping point? Nothing! With the camera on the photons remained particles. Without the camera the photons were waves and particles. As Morgan Freeman put it in his eloquent narration of the experiment:

"Think you know what reality is? Well, think again!"

Does this mean that you have no idea what is real and what is not? Yes it does!

Does it mean that you change your ideas of reality and the way it behaves just by looking at it? Yes, that is true!

If a tree falls in the woods and there is no one to see it, does the tree exist? The answer is yes and no. it doesn't exist because you didn't see or witness it. Yet it does exist because you can imagine the tree falling in your mind. So if someone puts the idea of a tree falling into your mind, your mind does the rest!

Does this mean that there is a virtual reality that you see as a physical reality? Yes it does.

This is very important for you to understand. All your life you have been given ideas, concepts and information about yourself that don't really exist. It is someone else's point of view on what reality should be like.

These ideas you have taken on board as if they were true and this has become the blueprint for how you live your life. What if none of it was true?

Concepts, ideas and information have been planted like a tree so firmly in your mind, you are beyond questioning them. It is just the same as saying the earth is flat.

These are very exciting times. You are now in the realms of science fiction, where everything is possible. Nothing is how it seems. Including you!

You are particles and waves. You are physical and you are virtual. When I think of my friend, George, he is just as real to me in my mind. He doesn't need to be standing in front of me.

Someone has given you information about you which you have then built on. Rather than dismiss or even update the information you have accepted it to be you. The information you hold about yourself in your virtual world has become your reality in the physical.

Let's explore the concept of you being particle and wave a little more.

Look at your hand right now. You can see that it is made up of particles. Let's look at your mind. You cannot see your mind. Where is it? It is there even though you cannot see it. It is your virtual reality that you are using to process information from what you are reading.

The fact that you cannot see the mind is part of the problem. If I cut my finger, I can see the blood. I can make a judgement whether to go to the hospital or not. I can take measures to look after the finger until it gets better. I also know that finger will never be the same again; it will always have a scar or suffer a weakness. Your finger will always be vulnerable.

What happens if you have an injury in your virtual world? Do you think that you can walk around bleeding all over yourself and everyone else? Do you think by ignoring the injury by some fluke the pain will go away? Do you think that others will not notice? By the way, injuries of the mind are low self-esteem. Lack of confidence. Stress. Worrying just about everything. Fear of just about everything.

You know, because the double slit experiment informs us, that you can change the way that reality behaves by changing the way that you look at it.

So let's go and change reality. Your brain is particle. Your mind is wave. Your brain is physical, your mind is virtual. Your brain is form and your mind is no form. You cannot be other than that because everything on the planet is so. Just because you cannot see certain things with the eye doesn't mean they don't exist. You cannot see the air that you breathe, yet you know it is vital to your existence.

Your mind, your virtual reality, is vast. It holds every piece of information about everything that has ever happened to you, big or small, everything! It also holds information about everything that you have witnessed but didn't actually happen to you. It holds information that you have overheard. It draws conclusions about everything. It holds information about you that is simply not true. Even if it was true back in the day, it is not true now.

Your virtual world

So you live in a physical world and a virtual world. In fact, you spend more time in your virtual world than you do in the physical. Your thoughts, beliefs, memory and experience reside in your mind, which you cannot see. The only time you can see a thought or an idea is when you transform it into reality by talking or doing something. You are an entire virtual universe hosted by planet Earth. Everyone is! Every element that you can find in the vast universe is represented or has the potential for representation in your body. The reason you don't produce diamonds is because you will not live long enough. Shame, eh?!

Just as a drop of water from the ocean still holds all the elements of the ocean, it is the same for you. You are a perfect replica of the bigger picture. Think of it like this; if the universe had a child, that child is you. Everything is there in perfect form and no form. Everything is there with potential.

Your virtual universe, which is called the mind, is made up of all your experiences that have happened to you or those that haven't happened to you which you have stored... just in case!

As a virtual universe you are sharing the planet with millions and millions of other virtual universes. Now, it would be very difficult for you to communicate with others if you were just a virtual entity with no form. How you communicate with another person is through a series of events that occur every minute of the day. These events you can call reality. Your virtual world and your physical world are inter-dependent.

Imagine you and I are walking down the road and you witness an accident. Even though you see the same event in the reality world, you and I will see the accident differently. It stands to reason in one sense. First, even though we may be walking down the road together, we do not see the same things. We are at different angles for one. Secondly, our virtual realities are at different levels of energy and vibration. If I didn't get any sleep the night before, my alertness will be impaired. I see the car from a different angle to you. In fact I see everything at a different angle to you. It stands to reason; I am not you and you are not me. How you experience things is your own special version of events and your interpretation of those events. If there were ten people at the scene of the accident, ten people would report something different. This is where lawyers come in, I guess!

Virtuality is like space itself; it is there and everywhere. Its nature is to   be one vast energy source. In order to experience 'life' on the planet it transforms itself into matter. This matter happens to be your body. In other words, your body is a capsule that hosts an entire universe. You are not a part of nature... you are nature!

The best analogy I can come up with to explain this phenomenon is this. Let's say you took a cupful of water from the ocean and put it in a glass container. That cupful of water still has all the elements of the ocean. It has ocean-like potential. That is to say, that all that could happen in the ocean could happen in your cup of water – only in miniature. The glass container is your body and the water inside your body has wave potential like the waves of the mighty ocean.

It is very difficult to get a grip on your virtual world. It is chaos. Ideas pop into your head with no rhyme or reason. You haven't thought about your old math's teacher for fifteen years and suddenly there you are thinking about her. How does that happen? You have never held a snake with your bare hands but suddenly the thought of a snake looms in your mind and you break into a cold sweat. What's going on?

You have no control over your thoughts and feelings. It is always hit and miss if you are going to be able to concentrate on something you really need to do. Your mind decides whether you will do stuff on time. The mind is lazy when you want to do something. It will come on with a million and one excuses why you shouldn't do stuff. But when you listen to your mind it will actually chastise you for not doing the very thing it told you not to do. Your mind never shuts off. It is always talking to you. Do this, don't do that. Think of this, don't think of that. Think about this person... I like this person... I don't like what they did...what am I going to do if...I should have, would have, could have, blah blah blah! Your motor is running endlessly...and you have misplaced the off switch. This means you are wasting energy!

Isn't it obvious that you are not alone in your virtual world? There are entities in there besides you, feeding you information. Who are they? What do they want? How did they get there?

Yes! It is true; you have dwellers in your mind. Your mind dwellers have taken over your show.

26

"Reality is merely an illusion, albeit a very persistent one."

~Chapter Three~

In The Beginning...

You were born with a blank sheet of paper for a mind. You knew nothing about the collective reality. You knew nothing about anything. All you were as a baby was a bubble of consciousness. You didn't know where you started or finished. You knew nothing, yet as far as you were concerned, you were the centre of the universe. A ball of energy! One by one, like foot soldiers, your senses started to formulate. You made contact. You experienced yourself, therefore, through your senses. You began to find out things about yourself, your status or lack of it in the collective reality. Your senses were your connection with the collective reality. The collective reality is your environment. Your senses are just that; sensors, observing and feeding back information so that you can make an informed decision.

If you want to get an idea of what is it is like to exist without your senses, then simply close your eyes and cover your ears and stand in the middle of your room for about five minutes. That is what it is like.

You have a body that houses your senses. Your senses tell you if anything is going on that you should know about. Your senses talks to your emotions and thoughts and you can actually internalise sensations into more feelings and thoughts. Your thoughts and feelings hit up against your beliefs and cultural perceptions about life and people.

You were born with no agenda other than to experience energy from the point of view of a human being. Instead of doing just that, something got lost in translation. Instead of being a part of the universe expressed in human form, with infinite potential, you become this bundle of flesh, raw nerves and jumbled and repetitive thoughts. How did that happen?

Well, it's like this.

When you were born, you had to be indoctrinated into the collective reality as soon as possible. Society can only tolerate a few free spirits and there cannot be people running up and down expressing themselves as they wish. More to the point, this idea of free will destroys the very premise of collective reality. If you have a collective reality, first people have to believe in it. They have to believe it is the best. They have to learn the rules. They have to understand what happens to them if they do not obey the rules. They have to understand that they have to defend this collective reality if it is attacked. To the death, if need be!

You have to learn and learn fast. What faster way but to give you a script? Learn your lines, play your part and don't step out of line. This script tells you exactly the role you will play in your life. All the people around you are also actors in your play.

All the major players tell you over and over again how to act out your role. They tell you what do. Stand here or there. Study. Eat. Talk, don't talk. Talk to them, don't talk to them.

You rehearse every day, hoping to be the star in your own play or hoping to get applause. Your job is never to question the play that you are in. Never challenge the role that you have been given. Do not misinterpret the script even if it makes the play seemingly better. Just learn your lines and get on with it. That is what you are told. That is what you believe... that is what you do.

Or do you...?

The cultural script is the first thing you have to learn. The culture is the backdrop or the setting for the play. The play by the way... is your life.

Cultural scripts are the accepted and expected patterns of behaviour that happen in a society. They can be overt like language and dress or they can be just below the surface, such as how men and women relate to each other. I remember when I worked in Saudi Arabia, I arrived at my hotel and decided, with my Western virtual world view that I would go out for a walk. Well, shut the back door! Women walking on the street *alone*! Unheard of!

I nearly caused a riot. I didn't speak the language, I had no idea why all these cars where beeping at me. Have you ever been in a traffic jam when one car starts beeping and then another starts beeping for no apparent reason? It was like that. There I was, walking down the road minding my own business and at the same time wondering why I was drawing so much attention to myself. I looked down at myself in my black robe that I was told to wear and for a while I thought:

"Hey Bev, you must be looking really good in this here *shaylah*; everyone is looking at you."

When I got to work the next day, I asked certain people why nearly every car was beeping at me. They casually told me that women were not allowed to walk the streets alone. I couldn't believe it. Yet the women there for the most part accept it! That's cultural scripts for you.

Every culture has a national personality, which everyone in that culture accepts to a more or lesser degree. The culture is a script that everyone within that culture knows by heart. The culture that you are born into just happens. You are required to play your part and that is it. If you play your part you'll be rewarded. If you try to rebel or step outside the box you will receive disapproval, ridicule or punishment, and so on. The culture may ostracise you or even kick you out.

How a culture keeps you in check is through your family. The culture is perpetuated through the family.

Your culture provides the backdrop for your play. It tells you the language, how to dress yourself, the ritual, the religion, the customs and pastimes, your position and expectation as a male or female. Whether you should like those people in that country or trust others who are different. It tells you everything so that you do not have to worry or think about it. Everything has been figured out for you and all you have to do, is play your part and without asking too many questions!

Oh, and there is nothing you can do about it. You can never escape your cultural script. It's like asking a leopard to change its spots. You cannot not be a Russian, Romanian, Chinese, American or a Jamaican. I myself don't like everything about my culture. I do not uphold many of the British so- called traditions. I can't tell you the last time I had tea and cucumber sandwiches at 4 pm. For all my disagreements with my culture, I am a British woman. My passport tells me I am British. My actions tell others that I am British. I say sorry for everything and my manners are impeccable. If I do something which steps outside of the British character norm my consciousness will kick me and reprimand me. I don't even think about the role I play every day. I have long since forgotten that I am playing a role. The role is playing me. Yet, if I didn't have my cultural script then who on earth would I be?

If there are any details that need to be filled out about your performance then your family will help you out. This is where Mum and Dad come in. Your parents tell you about the scope of the culture, the dos and don'ts, on a daily basis.

It is from them that you decide how important your role in the play really is. You get to understand the overt and covert expectations that they may have for you. They tell you if you are smart or dumb. They tell you if you are good looking or just so-so. They tell you your rightful place in the play and therefore in the collective reality. They feed you food and they feed you hope, your beliefs, your fears and your expectations. They program you so that you can in turn program others. They teach you how to separate from yourself and become selfless. To focus on yourself would be selfish.

Without realising it you develop a psychological script.

When you have developed a psychological script then your parents' job is more or less done. Apart from the odd prodding here and there, they feel good that they have delivered an upright member of the collective reality to the collective reality.

I want to say a little bit more about your script...

You use your radar to pick up all information about your environment and the people in it. You also get to pick up stuff about yourself.

There are messages said directly to you.

"You are beautiful."

"You are fat and lazy."

"You are so stupid."

Or worse... "Why are you so stupid?" (Don't you just hate it when asked to justify your own stupidity?)

There are messages that are said indirectly.

"Laura is so clever!"

"That Bev will never amount to much!"

"David has two left feet."

There are messages with inferences.

"Oh that girl over there is sitting so nice and still." (To be nice you need to sit still.)

"Look at Fred sharing his toys... what a good boy." (To share stuff is good so not to share is bad.)

"That's a good man. He is strong and brave." (In order to be a man you need to be strong at all times.)

"That's a great woman; she always does the right thing." (There is a right way and a wrong way to do things.)

The script is like stage directions. They tell you where to stand, how to stand how long to stand. If someone talks to you, it informs you where to put your hands. It tells you if you can touch and if you can't touch, what parts are acceptable to touch. In some scripts you may shake hands upon greeting; in others you may kiss the cheek. The script will even tell you how many times you may kiss the cheeks. In other scripts, you don't do any of the above

…you rub noses.

The biggest word that is used to get you to play a 'good role' is not a big word at all. It is one of those words that your mind doesn't know what to make of. The word is 'don't.'

Of course you understand what the word means intellectually, but when you tell me "don't do this or that" it creates confusion in my mind. Why? Because everything is possible in the virtual world. Everything is infinitely possible. You cannot say to energy "don't." What does the word "don't" mean to energy?

Here are just a few of the don'ts you encounter in your imprint years. Let's take a look at this deadly word 'don't' a little closer.

Don't #One:

"*Don't...*" –This 'don't' means just be fearful about pretty much anything and everything. These messages come from the Big People. The Big People is any adult that you know that you came into contact with when you were young. The Big People are over protective and so scared of messing up that they project all of those "don'ts" onto you.

"Don't run."

"Don't do that."

"Don't go too far."

"Don't climb that tree."

Later on in life it may become:

"Don't go for it." (The job, the relationship or whatever)

"Don't make plans."

"Don't step outside your comfort zone."

The Big People want to protect you from life, from others and from yourself. The world to them is a dangerous place and they need to pass this message on to you. This message is all about fear. If you listen to these messages you are afraid to live and enjoy your life. You are fearful that something is going to happen.

Don't # Two

"*Don't Be*" – in your script you may have picked up this message. That is, to tell you in another way that you were not wanted or your arrival was inconvenient. It never seizes to amaze me how mothers can talk about their offspring as if they have no ears. They *can* hear you!

"Oh, that's Johnny my youngest, he wasn't planned."

"If it weren't for you children, I could divorce your father…"

"You were a mistake."

"See what you do, why do you put me through this?!"

"I wish you'd never been born!"

If this is the message you constantly heard in your formative years you now suffer with not exactly fitting in.

Don't # Three

"*Don't Be Close*" – this message informs your script that physical and emotional closeness is a bad thing. You were encouraged not to get too close. There was a lack of affection or the affection given was awkward.

"Get off me, I'm busy."

"Don't touch me with your sticky hands."

"Leave me alone… I'm tired."

"You're too big to sit on my knee."

If you have picked up this message then getting close to people and letting your guard down will always be an issue for you. Your biggest fear is rejection and so you don't even try to get too close.

Don't # Four

"*Don't Be Important*" – This message comes from the belief in the collective reality that children are not important or that they have a limited status. This is not the case in every culture.

"Keep your mouth shut at the dinner table."

"If you don't be quiet I am going to give you to the gypsies."

"Children should be seen and not heard." (That was a particular favourite of my mother's.)

This message is very difficult to shake off. It means that you struggle to speak up for yourself. You don't think that what you have to say or what you do is of any significance. You litter your conversation with:

"It was nothing." (When, in fact, you slaved all day at something.)

"I'm only the office manager." (When, in essence, if it wasn't for you, nobody would have a clue how things get done.)

"It's only my opinion but…"

You dismiss yourself before you even open your mouth. You tell others your ideas only to find that they get the credit for them and not you.

Don't # Five

"Don't Be a Child" – As a child you may have been assigned the role of looking after your brothers and sisters while your mother and father went out to work. This certainly was the case for me.

"Oh grow up."

"Act your age."

"Don't talk nonsense."

"Don't be so childish."

"Hello little man."

"You're a proper little madam, aren't you?"

I was always told that I had to take care of my younger sister. Even when my sister was grown with a family of her own, my mother would still say to me that I had to "look out for my sister." Inside I always wondered who it was that was looking out for me. If you picked up this message as I did, then you always have to be the strong and the sensible one. People look to you for guidance and always find you when they need something for you to sort out.

Don't # Six

"*Don't Grow Up*" – The youngest member of the family usually gets this message. No matter how old you become, you are always the baby of the family and so it is hard for you to be taken seriously. Whatever you do you will be criticised because of the very strong expectation for you to never grow up.

"He's the baby of the family."
"You're Daddy's little girl."
"No one is good enough for my little girl."

Don't # Seven

Don't Succeed" –This is an interesting message. It could have a number of meanings. First, it could be "don't be successful" so that you don't step out of line. In other words, know your place. Second, it could mean be successful, but don't be too successful because then it will seem as if you are showing off. Always play your achievements down. Third, there could be a message saying be successful by all means, but do not be more successful than me. You don't want people to become jealous of success; that would make *them* feel uncomfortable and that wouldn't do.

"We are engineers in this family and you want to be a what? A dancer? Are you mad?"
"People like us do not go to university."
"I told you it would never happen."
"They don't give jobs to people like you."
"What! You want to do what… are you mad?"

35

Don't # Eight

"*Don't Be You*" – In this collective reality, the Big People feel that the best way to induct you is to try and get you to be like someone else.

"Why don't you sit still like Amy?"

"Why don't you get good grades like Jeff?"

"I'm sure Sophie's parents don't have this problem with her."

Sometimes the Big People are given boys but they long for girls or vice versa, so they ignore the sex of the child and dress them up in the clothes they want, like little dollies or even a 'mini me'.

A mother with four boys who wanted a girl may subconsciously make the youngest one her "daughter". Or a father with all girls may make one of them a "little buddy" by giving positive strokes for doing son-like activities.

Don't # Nine

"*Don't Be Sane*" – Children who grow up with Big People who have a mental illness can learn how to 'do' mental illness through role modelling. They may also get negatively stroked for healthy thinking and positively stroked for silly or bizarre behaviours. Most often, double-bind messages from the Big People to a child where the child is 'damned if s/he does and damned if s/he doesn't' can foster this distorted reality.

Don't # Ten

"*Don't Be Well*" – Once when I was nine years old, I became very ill with bronchitis. The doctor was called and he suggested that I stay in bed for at least a week. Well, I was suddenly the queen of the castle. My sister and everyone were at my beck and call. For one week I could eat anything. Stay in bed and read comics. It was perfect. Apart from the odd coughing up of a lung it was heaven. To be honest it was the only time in my family when I felt important. Luckily for me that wasn't my script to believe that the only way to get attention is to be sick. Doctors have a name for it. They call it the "worried well" – these are people who as soon as you as you start a conversation will proceed to tell you about their aches and pains and ailments.

Some children only experience nurturing when they are sick. They grow up to use the sick role to gain the attention of others and to self-nurture as well. Usually at a subconscious level, getting well would mean isolation and abandonment to someone with this message.

Don't # Eleven

"*Don't Belong*" – As a child I had a number of new addresses. It was very difficult to make friends as I was constantly moving on. I was rich pickings for the local neighbourhood bully. I had about six 'first days' at school. Always the newbie and always wondering what the hell was going on.

"Class, let me introduce Bev, the new girl... I need someone to volunteer to look after her." At this point the whole class would physically groan at the prospect.

"We don't do it like that here."

"I swear I don't know where he came from?" (Laughter)

Don't # Twelve

"*Don't Talk*" – I think everyone gets this message to a more or lesser extent from their family. The Big People in the family decide what you can talk about and what topics are off limits. The topics of conversation then become the family currency. It is like a sort of code that only the family know about. How you get to find out what is on or off are by the facial expressions of your Big People. Good stuff is rewarded by smiles and responsiveness and bad things get frowns and silence.

What was OK to talk about in the family?

Was it OK to talk about what was going on in other people's lives, like the neighbours, but it was not OK to talk about feelings and emotions in the family?

Because...

"If I don't talk about it then it won't hurt and will go away."

"Why do you always have to bring that up?"

"Stop it... you know how that kind of talk upsets your mother."

"No one knows how to raise the subject."

Don't # Thirteen

"*Don't Trust*" – With this 'don't', you learn very quickly, usually from the actions of your family, that people are not to be trusted. Your family demonstrate this over and over again, either by their actions or their pains to point out others' indiscretions. You learn that if you trust no one you will never be disappointed.

"I'm sorry; we can't go to the zoo... Daddy has to work late." (Again)

"I don't know when I'm coming back."

"Don't bother me now; I'm talking to Jane (friend) on the phone. We'll play later." (Later never comes)

Don't # Fourteen

"*Don't Feel what you feel, or only feel what I feel or if you feel too much you are out of control.*" In order to belong to a collective reality, you have to figure out which feelings to save and which ones to delete; which ones are

38

the good guys and which ones are the bad guys. In most collective realities, an extreme demonstration of emotion is out of the question. Any overuse of emotions is distasteful, even if they are positive ones. There is a saying that the Big People say in Britain that is very freaky.

"What are you smiling at? I'll wipe that smile off your face."

Or, this one is even more terrifying:

"You'll be smiling at the back of your head if you are not careful."

You are told that getting too excited about anything is not a very good thing. Being too pleased with yourself is equally bad. So, you learn not to 'big up' your achievements and talents.

If someone tells you that you have done a good job, you learn to tell yourself that "It was nothing."

If you show any of the emotions that are not allowed you will cause great embarrassment to your Big People, as everyone will be able to see that they are not doing a good job in inducting you into the collective reality. People will question their skills or worthiness to be parents and Big People.

"What will other people think?"

"You are showing me up."

"Come on, you're making a fool of yourself."

"Get a grip…"

In order to show that you are coming along nicely and ready for the collective reality, it is important for you to 'dumb down' and in some causes 'numb' your emotions. Depending on the collective reality and their emotional tolerance to emotions, you are told that to be emotional is to be 'out of control.'

"What's got into you?"

"You're talking nonsense right now."

You are told that there must be a reason for your emotional response.

"You're not yourself today… you must be tired!"

"You always get irritable when you are hungry"

"Are you sad ... don't be sad, it's all for the best!"

Others in the collective reality constantly tell you what to think.

"You must be very annoyed with him."

"You should have given her a piece of your mind."

"You shouldn't have let him get away with that."

The common belief is that in time the offending emotion will dissipate and you will no longer need it. Well, you know that is not true. What do you think happens to any energy if you block it? People suffer from 'emotional intolerance to emotion'; what I mean by this is because people are not allowed to deal with their emotions and thus develop emotional intelligence, when emotions get high, as they have a habit of doing, people think that the best way to deal with them is to get emotional as well.

When that happens, people talk about the situation getting out of hand or that it is very emotional. In the collective reality, to show any out of the norm emotion is out of order. The Big People don't know how to respond. They worry that the emotion is contagious and that they may catch it, thus showing that they are out of control.

Depending again upon your collective reality, you may be inducted by the Big People telling you what to feel and how to feel.

"If I were you I would be upset by that."

"You must be really angry."

"Put your coat on, you must be cold."

Sometimes a raw emotion can sift through the net and cause people to get emotional.

This happens when world events like 9/11 or the death of Princess Diana cause the emotion of grief to burst out. Because everyone in the collective reality is feeling it to some degree, it is allowed for a while.

In order for you to conform and become a model human you have to learn the 'don'ts'. 'Don't' is a good word to use. It is simple for you to understand. It is also effective in that it creates the right amount of confusion in your virtual reality. It is the only word that is effective enough to plant the necessaries required for you to operate in the collective reality without causing a scene. Let's just spend a moment to see how the word 'don't' works.

For the next ten seconds I don't want you to think of a pink elephant wearing a bikini. Got it? Don't think of the pink elephant wearing the bikini. It's amazing and frightening to see how this word allows the information to slide in without challenge. Instead of thinking to yourself "Why can't I think of a pink elephant?" or "That's right, I do not want to think of an elephant right now", you find that you actually can't stop thinking of the pink elephant. The word 'don't' allows the instruction, belief, value, message, opinion to go inside your system without protest or alarm. You eat your food. You digest the don'ts. Simple indoctrination.

Can you imagine how many rules you have taken on board in your life without question? They just slide into your psyche without a bye or leave. You do not know why you do half the things you do, you just do.

You just say to yourself, that's the way I am. Is it? Is it really? Who said that?

What about the concept of free will? Do you have no say in the matter?

The concept of free will is an interesting one and that free radical has to be tamed very quickly. Sometimes during your imprint years you may have tried to exercise your free will. Just to test your boundaries. In the process of discovering who you are, your free will wants to express itself because that was your nature to do things at will, spontaneously and just because...

Your free will decides that it doesn't want to put a jacket on to go outside. Your free will may even put up a fight but in the end it succumbs to the pressure of the Big People.

Your free will realises that it is not you that holds the power and control over you and falls silent.

Let me give you a scenario so you can see how the free will is broken down and sent packing.

You: "I don't like peas."

Big People: "They are good for you."

You: "I still don't like them."

Big People: "You will learn to like them."

You: "I will not... I hate them."

Big People: "You will sit there until you eat them."

You: "O.K."

Big People: "Believe me, there is no more food."

You: "O.K." (Perhaps a little too defiantly)

Big Person: "If you don't eat them now you will get them again for breakfast, dinner and tea."

You: "O.K."

Big Person: "I can't believe you are being so rude."

You: "I just don't like them… they taste funny."

Big Person: "Don't be ridiculous…they taste fine to me…you know what the starving children would do for those peas."

You: "So why don't you send them the peas."

Big Person: "Such insolence. You don't know how I suffer at work to put food on the table... go to your room... and don't come out until you change your tune …"

You: "Sorry."

Big people: "Sorry for what?"

You: "Sorry for not liking peas."

Big People: "No, sorry for being so ungrateful and rude."

In this scenario, Big People use guilt, starvation, solitary confinement and character assassination to get you to eat peas.

I have a friend, who to this day will not eat peas or fish due to the test of wills he endured during his imprint stage.

After learning all about the 'don'ts', you have to learn the 'do's'.

42

You are told if you do any or all of the following, you will be O.K.

So you learn to be strong, perhaps never letting people get close to you or show any emotions.

You learn to be a perfectionist, never letting things go because you are told that your best is not good enough.

You learn to try hard, and that if you just keep trying maybe someone, somewhere will have pity on you and let you stick around.

You learn to always be in a hurry. If you want something done ask a busy person, and that is you. You learn to be super-efficient. Multi-tasking is your middle name!

You learn to please others. You hate conflict or rocking the boat. You become over concerned with what other people think.

You live your life carefully. Sometimes you have dreams of travelling, but you have been told over and over again that it is a dangerous world out there. You are careful with everything, and I mean everything. You weigh things up; you know every risk analysis theory in the book. It is impossible for you to make a decision. Your favourite phrase to yourself is: "What if". You decide you have to work hard to justify your existence. Nothing is too much for you to take on. You become over loaded and stressed out at times, but you are just a person who just can't say "no".

Just a thought here... What happens if the Big People responsible for you get it wrong? What happens if the dos get mixed up with the don'ts?

Have you ever come across someone who always seems to go to the limit in life? Someone who drinks the party dry of alcohol, or someone who is always getting into trouble in some form or fashion?. Could it be that they got the messages all wrong and what they received was a mash up of "Don't... be careful" or "Don't think...drink" or Don't feel" or "Be strong, even if it kills you!" It kind of explains the unexplainable behaviour in some folk, doesn't it?

Here's another thought... what happens if you are inducted by Big People who have conflicting views as to what to do with you? One says, "Don't be stupid" and the other says, "Use your brain." One says, "I can't wait for you to settle down with some nice person," and the other says, "Get a career." One says, "It's good to have friends," and the other says, "Trust nobody."

Here's another thought... what happens when the Big People instruct you to do something but you observe them doing the exact opposite? Don't speak with your mouth full. They do that. Don't smoke, they say. They do that. Don't tell lies, they say. They do that.

All of these mixed, unclear and confusing messages are not conducted deliberately... I repeat: they are not deliberate. They are done outside of our awareness, but in the end they make you unsure. If you are unsure, you always live with self-doubt. If you live with self-doubt, you never have the confidence to question or to break the mould. If you never have the confidence to break the mould when it is time for you to have children and when it is time for you to induct them into the collective reality, you know exactly without doubt what you have to do. The collective reality can therefore continue unchallenged. In order to have a collective reality, people need to believe in the collective.

In the imprint stage, you learn a great deal about yourself. Everything you know about yourself has been taught. In other words, you are someone else's opinion. However, it only matters when you click the button and 'accept'. No one forces you to accept.

Stories abound of people being told by the Big People that they would never amount to anything and they have proven them wrong. Some people reject the script they have been given, mainly because a stronger or more inviting script reveals itself at a crucial time.

44

Carlos Acosta, the principal dancer at the National Ballet in England, and a world renowned ballet dancer, was introduced to ballet by his father as a punishment and also in desperation. Carlos was born in the backstreets of Havana, Cuba. He had no money and no future. He spent most of his days causing trouble in the neighbourhood. His father put him in ballet class as a way of calming him down and to teach him a lesson. His father also thought that Carlos would become a bit of a laughing stock in the gang when they found out that he attended ballet class and so lose his status within the gang. Who knew that Carlos was going to be brilliant? In the dilapidated streets of Havana, Carlos found dance and chose a different script for himself.

Especially during the imprint period, you are in somewhat of a perpetual hypnotic state. Your brain is like a sponge that soaks in everything the Big People tell you.

Attributions are the frequent comments made by the Big People, which plant 'post-hypnotic' suggestions in the mind of a child. For example, when mother says the following:

"Susie tries hard but she is just not very good at homework, are you dear?"

"Bobby may not be showing it right now, but he is very smart and he is going to show everyone just how smart, isn't that right Bobby?"

You have little choice but to answer "Yes" to the tag question at the end of the statement. This and the repetition are what lock the attribution in place.

So first, you accept the messages as a way of defining yourself. Second, you press play and you start to act out your script accordingly. Third, you have to justify your decision to yourself, so here are some of the justifications you make.

"Don't..." -- *"I can't decide, so I need someone to decide for me."*

"Don't Succeed" -- *"I can't do anything right." "So I'm*

stupid." "So I'll never win anything."

"Don't Be Well or Sane" -- *"So I must be crazy." "My condition is beyond hope, I can never get better."*

"Don't Feel" -- *"Emotions are a waste of time, what's the point?" "Showing emotion is a sign of weakness. People will take advantage if you show emotion." "I'm an emotional wreck."*

"Don't Feel That" -- *"I'm never angry... anger is dangerous" "You wouldn't like me if I got angry, so I'm just going to bury my feelings." "I won't let my emotions get the better of me."*

"Don't Feel What You Feel...Feel What I Feel" -- *"I don't know what I feel." "So how should I feel?" "How would you feel, if you were me?"*

Because you were this bundle of consciousness, you were able to pick up things about you fast. You pick up the body language. Apart from things said to you directly or indirectly, you pick up stuff said to others that has something in the message for you. You pick up information from the fairy stories. You pick up information from the history of your collective reality to find out who are the guys that get praised and become heroes and who are the guys that get into trouble. You learn who the archetypes are for everyone from hero to foe. You develop models in your virtual mind about what a relationship, a career, a body is, and what their ingredients are. You then set your chin to the wind and go out in search of these models in the collective reality. You develop patterns and a way of thinking, feeling and being that becomes your blueprint. Against this blueprint you therefore define yourself. If you didn't have this blueprint then who on earth would you be? All of this, so that you can be the model human being and a robot.

Common sense is the collection of prejudices acquired by age eighteen."

~Chapter Four~

Your Indoctrination

Now let's look at the virtual world you call your mind. Imagine that your virtual world was in fact a house. A house is a little more manageable to get your head around than the universe right now.

In your house you have some housemates. These housemates of yours are very important because they keep you in touch with reality or let's call it the reality you share with others. This reality I call the collective reality. Your housemates keep a very watchful eye on what's going on out there and report back to the others. The others then decide how they should feel, react and what, if anything, they should do. They bring up issues from the past to bring evidence as to why you should feel or do something. They control you. It doesn't matter if what is happening out there is not that bad, they filter the information, so that by the time they have finished with it, you have nothing to do but go along with whatever they say. They will cause you to worry or even fixate on an issue until another issue comes up which more is pressing. Issue files on top of issue. Unfinished business. They are not in the business of problem solving and moving on. No, they prefer to store information, beliefs, assumptions and perceptions in order to bombard you into submission at a later event.

This isn't such a bad thing really, only that they have developed ideas above their station. Instead of deferring to you, you now defer to them. How did that happen?

As I say, they are your connection with the collective reality out there. They are the guys that keep you connected with the planet, so you can't get rid of them, as tempting as it may seem. Wouldn't it be nice to just lop off

47

the bits of you that didn't work? Just think about it, if one of your fingers didn't work properly. Let's say you woke up one day and it was swollen and stiff. What would you do, go get a knife and cut it off? No, I don't think so!

You would probably try to analyse the problem to see if you could fix it. All the digits that make up your hands work both independently of each other and together, so each of them is valid and necessary for you to do stuff. You probably don't realise how necessary each finger is until something happens to one of them.

So is the case for your housemates. They work independently of each other and they work together. They don't work all the time but they do keep a lazy eye on what's going on in the collective reality just to keep tabs on your performance out there. If there is a so-called crisis then they start talking and bring up evidence from the past to strengthen their arguments and their position.

Oh, by the way, the arguments do not have to be logical or even make sense. Their job is to keep you safe. They think that the way to do this is to keep you separated from things or how things work, so they can deal with you as an individual. It's like a divide and rule policy. If they isolate you then you will feel vulnerable. If you feel vulnerable and small you will become even more dependent on their whims and wiles. It soon becomes you against the rest of the world. Actually, it is more like this: you and your unruly housemates against the world. No, actually, it is more like this: your out of control housemates against you and the world.

Now, you may have difficulty relating to the concept that there are housemates living inside your mind that have got a little bit out of control. It is a leap, I will grant you that…just bear with me a little longer…

Let's run a simple experiment right now!

Tell yourself you are going to the gym.

Say, "I am going to the gym." If you do not belong to a gym then tell yourself you are going outside for a run…

And wait…

What's happening? Nothing…OK, go and put your trainers on… and wait...

This is probably what will happen next…

"You can't go out now." (A voice)

"It's very late and it looks like rain..." (A concerned voice)

"It looks scary outside" (A worried voice)

"Didn't some woman get mugged the other day?" (A scared voice)

Just imagine how great you will feel if you actually go!" (An excited voice)

"Remember the pain you had in your knee the last time you did something stupid like go out for a run on concrete..."(A condescending voice)

"You haven't got the right gear … you can't possibly go out, what will the neighbours think?" (An embarrassed voice)

Now say to yourself, "I am not going to go to the gym or out for a run"....and wait…

Ten minutes later.

"Why didn't you go for a run?"

"You are so lazy…" (A disgusted voice)

"You're never going to lose that weight." (A resigned voice)

"You are a fat slob." (An angry voice)

"You may as well eat that cheesecake in the fridge or it will go to waste." (A hopeless voice)

"Why don't you go for a run tomorrow?" (A hopeful voice)

And that is how it is in your head. Day and night. Chattering about everything. Droning on about every event. Sometimes you can't even get to sleep because of all the noise. Nothing gets past those guys. Imagine if the fingers on your hand did that, you would never do anything! Before you decided to pick something up, each finger would give you an individual and unique

49

assessment of the situation, spelling out dangers past, present and future. Spelling out issues that have happened to you or happened to others or issues they have seen on T.V. The little finger talks to the middle finger, the thumb interjects. The index finger brings up stuff from the past. The forefinger is pointing and the other fingers wag. They shout, talk over each other and they don't listen at all. If this was the case how long would it take you to do the smallest of things?

This is what is going on in your head. It is noisy and overcrowded and you are exhausted.

So let's take a look at these guys that occupy your head space.

They take up residence from the moment you are born. They are there for the good reason that they are the ones that look outside your virtual world and report back to you and the other housemates what is going on, so you can know how to best participate in it. That is it! With this information, you can make an informed decision as to what to do with your life. It all goes a bit wrong when instead of informing you they give you their version of things and moreover give you their opinion of what you should do.

You have been inducted into your collective reality by the Big People. When you were a child, particularly in the Imprint Stage, which is between the ages of zero to seven, you were like a sponge. You ingested information from everywhere. You wanted to know who you were. You wanted to know who you were in relation to the Big People and you wanted to know how to get along with these people. Mostly, you wanted to belong. The ability for you to take in information at that age was phenomenal. At that time you were pure consciousness.

I don't know if you have ever watched the film *The Matrix*. In a nutshell, the main character Neo is chosen to save the world from the bad guys who are sucking the energy out of people and turning them into batteries. In order to be ready for the task ahead, he has to learn stuff at great speed. You are pretty much the same. You went through an indoctrination process which enabled you to join the collective reality, but instead of doing it in one hour and 45 minutes like the movies; you have all your life. The indoctrination process for you goes like this.

Zero – seven: *Imprint stage*. This is where all the beliefs, values and traditions of the collective reality are passed on to you.

Seven to 12: This is the *Modelling stage*. In this stage you are put on show and encouraged to show model behaviour. You may also be given role models and archetypes to aspire to.

13–18: This is the *Social stage*. In this stage you go out and test yourself against the others within your collective reality. That is to say, you compare yourself with others to gauge your status and worthiness. Fitting in is most important in this stage. It is true to say that your consciousness may   make a bid for freedom. You may rebel. You may want to express yourself as an individual with your hair, your music, your views, your clothes. The Big People are relentless in bringing you back into the fold. You have to eat by the clock, not when you are hungry. You have to study but you are never taught how to learn. You have to fit in and not create too much fuss.

So what happens after 18? You are an adult. And you are let loose in the collective reality to recreate the status quo. All the Big People that influenced your formative years are no longer around. If they are still around, they certainly cannot tell you what to do. Or can they?

How can the collective reality ensure that you have learnt what you need to learn to be an upright pillar of the establishment?

Well in two ways actually….

The first thing is that the Big People never go away. There is always someone bigger than you. It just depends how you define 'big'. There will be someone younger or older than you. There will be someone richer or poorer than you. There will be someone thinner, better looking, fitter, with longer hair, more travelled, better educated, with a better boyfriend or girlfriend. You name it, as I say it all depends on how you define big. All these Big People who have more of what you want. You compare and contrast yourself against these Big People on a daily basis. You beat yourself up if you fall short and most of the time you do, because there is always someone bigger and better. The Big People show you that the only way to achieve in the collective reality is if you are smart, work hard, try hard, are skinny, beautiful (according to the prescribed conditions of beauty), strong and able to do things to perfection.

They say:

"Losers never win."

"If at first you don't succeed, try, try and try again."

"Only the strong survive."

"The perfect size is size zero."

"Failure is not an option."

The collective reality is controlled by people reminding you how to be. If you step out of line, they will soon put you back on course. Don't believe me? Try doing something which is not considered the norm in your collective reality. Tell a friend you are going to quit your job. Or go to Africa to help out.

I will bet you a pound to a cent or a dollar to a penny cent that for every positive comment they give you, they will give you ten negative ones. Talk of leaving the collective reality is always discouraged!

So, there you are. You have accepted the script and now all you have to do is press play. When you press play the script runs in your head on a loop, as if on tapes, until the day you die. The collective reality reflects to you how you should behave and that is verified by the script playing in your head. If the information from the collective reality does not match the script version of things then the script will change reality to make it match. You live in a collective reality and a distorted version of the collective reality.

Wow! This is a lot to take in so let me give a small example of this.

Let's say that Jenny doesn't think very highly of herself.

During her imprint days she was told that she wasn't as good as her older sister, Jess. She was told that she should try to be just like her sister. Jenny loved her sister and at the same time she hated her. Jess was the source of her discomfort. To get away from the bad feelings she had about her sister, Jenny decided to be a perfectionist. She hoped for the day when people would recognise her for who she was. That day never comes. Whatever people say she doesn't believe them. This only made Jenny work even harder. In later life Jenny succeeds to the top of her field. Everyone tells her how brilliant she is. Jenny is driven by the voices in her head that tell her that she isn't good enough.

When the script locks in, it becomes what you call your personality. It's just the way you are. The personality is your interface between the collective reality and your virtual reality. Your personality is made up of all the points of views of the Big People.

No one has a personality that is one dimensional. Personalities are multi- faceted. You talk of:

"It seems she has a split personality."

"He doesn't have much of a personality."

"When I am at work I do not let that aspect of my personality show."

When I say to you that you have a stomach, kidneys and a liver inside your body, you know that is true. You have never seen your own kidneys, yet you know you have them. You don't know exactly what they do and how they do their job. You have seen pictures of what they are supposed to look like, so you know that they are there.

What if I said to you that inside your head you have some dwellers? They are there as sure as your kidneys are there.

These dwellers are the keepers of the script. They translate your beliefs and values from your virtual world into thoughts and then into behaviour in the collective reality. They translate behaviour in the collective reality into thoughts that reinforce who you are. Everything that happens in the collective reality must be filtered, washed, rearranged and even distorted by your personality to fit your perception of reality. Everything that you feel and think must be vetted by the personality to see if it is a match with who you think you are.

If you do not check and re-check on an hourly basis, the dwellers remind you that your behaviour doesn't actually fit their idea of who you are.

"What has possessed you to do that?"

"What's got into you these days?"

"Are you feeling yourself lately?"

"You're acting very strange lately... what's the matter?"

"I don't know how to take you."

All of these comments tell you that you are acting out of sorts with the collective reality and you'd better get back with the program.

What causes you to self-regulate and stay with the program every single day? What causes you to stick with the way that you are even when there is no one else around to challenge you? Who is it that talks you out of doing stuff or never finishing stuff off? Who is it that stops you from speaking up or speaking out? Who are these voices in your head?

Let me introduce you to the dwellers who I call your housemates. They are the voices in your head that make sure that you don't do anything rash. You defined yourself and they make sure that you stay true to that definition. If you decide to do anything which is out of keeping with your script you will be brought to task by your

54

housemates.

There are 12 housemates.

They are divided into lower ranking, middle ranking and then there are the big guns.

The lower ranking housemates are: Archetypes, Nurturing Parent, Identity, Free Child, Beliefs and Cognitive Dissonance. They are low ranking because they do not have a lot of power in the house amongst the other more high ranking housemates. Mostly they chatter and take up space.

The middle ranking housemates are Critical Parent, Adapted Child and Little Professor.

These three have a symbiotic relationship and they feed off each other. These are the foot soldiers who keep the system going. They constantly remind you of the rules so that you will not stray and do something out of the norm ordained for you. They take up a lot of psychic space.

Then we have the high ranking housemates. They are Emotions and Ego. They consider themselves very important. They demand space and they steal space. In every institution there is a manager or a boss to whom everyone must answer. The house is no different. Everyone bows to the highest ranking housemate of all. He is called Shame. If that wasn't enough to be getting on with you have the housemates' assistants. These are the guys that translate the 'goings on' in your house into behaviour in the collective reality. All the housemates use guerrilla tactics to be seen and heard. They hold you hostage and to ransom when you dare to do anything other than what they say.

So let's go meet the housemates…

"Small is the number of people who see with their eyes and think with their mind."

~Chapter Five~

Low Ranking Housemates

Housemate LR #1 – Archetypes

I am presenting the lower ranking housemates in no particular order.

Meet housemate number one. Your archetypes! He represents the assumptions that you have installed in your head of how a perfect life should be. They are assumptions that are developed by the Big People and fairy stories.

"One day my prince will come."

An archetype could be anything. It is your view of what perfect is. You have a view of what a perfect relationship should be like. In your head you have figured out the perfect partner for you. The looks, the height, the income, the intelligence, sense of humour, sensitivity and kindness. The lot! You have the picture drawn in your head of what a perfect partner looks and sounds like; now all you have to do is find the perfect match in the collective reality. How hard can it be? You have pictures on all the walls in your head of all your archetypes. Everything! You are either going to marry an avatar or a super hero. The problem is that not many super heroes visit your collective reality and you spend a lot of your time being disappointed with what's on offer.

"I like him but he's just a bit short for my liking."

"He's not good enough for you."

"I like a woman who is independent and strong."

"Lonely heart seeks Nobel peace prize winner."

I digress, I know, but I have to say this here. Just in case I forget. I was driving out with friends one day. Suddenly Jo piped up and said that she was going home to construct a 'mood board'. This was a revelation to me. I had heard about 'mood boards' in interior design. This is where you gather all sorts of colours, prints and textures to get ideas about how you want your house to look. Jo actually explained that she wanted to construct her perfect partner. She was actually going home to design a partner! Can you sense my incredulity? Now I had heard it all! I asked her how it worked. She told me that she had seen the film. I am not going to disclose the name of the film. These people have made enough money and they do not need help from me. Anyway, the film said that if you focus on something hard and long enough then your desires will come true. So during the car journey I quizzed Jo about her perfect partner. She went on to explain a person, who I think could heal the sick and cook dinner at the same time. This person was amazing. She was getting excited about it all. After she had finished her lengthy description, I said:

"Jo, you have just described the most amazing person, my question is how amazing are you? How do you rate against the criteria you have set for this person? If you are less than amazing why would that person want to be with you?"

Silence. She obviously hadn't heard of the laws of correspondence.

Oh and by the way, I hear she hasn't had any luck yet! Strange that!

Back to what I was talking about.

You have a picture of the perfect: job, car, house, cat, person, friends, Christmas, holiday, length of time waiting in a queue, neighbour, meal, T.V program, government, sunset, ice cream, and toilet paper. Need I go on? You have an archetype of everything. The fact that you have an opinion on everything and how everything should be is just what the Big People want. It is not open-minded. It is closed mindedness and it keeps you stuck!

Housemate LR #2 – Nurturing Parent

When I think of this housemate I am always reminded of a senior nurse. She is the housemate that looks after you. She likes to offers advice, support and protection. She is the side of you that is empathetic towards yourself and to others. In the collective reality she is concerned for others and in the virtual universe she is the voice that tells you to eat properly and get enough sleep.

"Don't worry about it."

"All you can do is your best."

"Have an early night and things will seem better in the morning."

"What you need is a nice cup of tea." (In my case, she always suggests wine.)

The matron doesn't have much say in the house and she is usually overruled by the other noisy, boisterous housemates who feel they know better. You have reduced her to a nagging voice at the back of your mind. You say to yourself.

"I know I should get more exercise but…"

"I know I should eat better but…"

"I know I should take better care of myself but…"

"I know I should value myself more…"

There's always a 'but' – why do you not put yourself first?

Housemate LR #3 – Free Child

This housemate is one of those guys that is the life and soul of the party. There is never a dull moment when this housemate is around. He is creative and spontaneous. He is affectionate and fun loving. In other words, what you see is what you get. He doesn't care about showing his feelings, whether they are positive or blocked. He is the part of you that the Big People set out to tame and control. He represents that side of you that is uncensored, free, curious, open, trusting, sensuous and natural. Just before you start to think that this housemate is too good to be true, he isn't. As with all free spirits, he can be self-centred and selfish. If this housemate was left up to their own devices, they would just want to play video games all day long and eat junk food.

"I've got a brilliant idea."

"Let's go out tonight and let our hair down!"

"Wow, that's an amazing car."

"I don't give a rat's arse what other people think."

"You only live once... so what the hell."

He is the side of you that represents your natural and carefree self. Some people have had their free child stunted to the point that they don't know how to have fun. Everything is serious. Life is a task. The only way for these people to let their hair down is to drink a lot or take drugs.

Housemate LR #4 – Identity

Identity is the housemate I am talking to when I ask you:

"Who are you?"

He is the guy that has internalised all the rules and regulations from the Big People. He is the guy that monitors and regulates everything you do in the collective reality. He does such an efficient job that the Big People don't even need to be around anymore. Your identity picks up the baton and continues with the job. He is the guy that defines you.

"I am shy."

"I am not confident."

"I'm too old/young."

"It's only my opinion but…"

"I am me."

Through a process of elimination you have defined yourself as this and not that.

"I couldn't do that…so I must be this."

59

"It's not me."

"I am ambitious."

"I wish I could do that…"

The point about Identity as a housemate is that he is not your true identity. He identifies with things and labels and not with representing who you are. He is a lower ranking housemate because he is weak.

Housemate LR #5 – Beliefs

This housemate represents what you have come to believe in. Your beliefs are the walls of your house and they hold everything up.

For any belief to have a power you have to believe in the belief. So the job of Beliefs is to make sure that your vision of the collective reality conforms to the beliefs that you have internalised about yourself and the world.

Let's say that you believe or you have come to believe that:

"People are not to be trusted."

What happens to your belief system if people in the collective reality demonstrate that they are trustworthy?

What does your belief system do then? It has to invent a reason for this. Maybe, they are being trustworthy as part of a cunning plan, and you should watch out!

Of course over time someone will do something 'wrong' where the belief system can then say:

"I told you so… people are not to be trusted."

The belief system housemate invents their own set of rules to keep people out.

"People are not to be trusted and so they have to work very hard to earn my trust."

"He's being nice to me… to gain my trust… what does he really want from me?"

What are beliefs anyway? They are your opinions. They are your interpretation of the rules. Some Big People take it upon themselves to make the rules as rigid as possible so that there is no room for manoeuvre.

"All women drivers are rubbish."

"All people from that country are thieves."

If you have opinions about anything or anyone, chances are they are wrapped up in a belief. A belief that is probably not yours anyway! You are the ventriloquist dummy spouting stuff which is hardly original or well thought out and in some cases just not true. You mindlessly repeat the beliefs as if they are laws. You are in danger of becoming just like a Big Person.

Housemate LR #6 – Cognitive Dissonance

Cognitive Dissonance is the name of this housemate. The definition of cognitive dissonance is two pieces of opposing information residing in you at the same time.

It's the wife of the abuser who knows she should leave and at the same time tries to justify her husband's behaviour. It is the knowing of something and the denial of the very thing that you know.

Another great example is, knowing that smoking is bad for you on the one hand and at the same time justifying why you smoke. I have a friend who has smoked since she was 13. Every year around January, she vows that she will never smoke another cigarette again. Come February, she is smoking like the proverbial chimney. I have challenged her in the past but now I just let her be; as long as she doesn't smoke in my house, I'm fine. I can't imagine the stress that her mind and body goes through every time she lights up a cigarette. She betrays herself. There are faster ways to kill yourself, I know, but what I think about is the amount of mental energy required to do something that you have told yourself you do not want to do.

You do it to yourself every day; knowing that you can do something and at the same saying that you can't do it.

I spend most of my working life working through people's cognitive dissonance. My job is to tell people they can, when they tell me they can't.

The opposing view, depending how strong the views are, vies for poll position, pulling at your very limbs, rendering you speechless when you need a voice, rendering you helpless when you need your strength, rendering you indecisive at the very point when you need to make a decision. Even making you say "Yes" when you are thinking "No". It is thinking overload until you get to the point when you have a thinking meltdown and nothing makes sense.

"Great spirits have often encountered violent opposition from weak minds."

~Chapter Six~

Middle Ranking Housemates

I now want to introduce the mid ranking housemates, thus called because they have powers in the house and the other housemates take their comments on board sometimes.

Housemate MR #1 – Critical Parent

This is the guy who has ingested everything about your culture and all that those Big People wanted for you in the imprint period of your development. His job is to defend the culture, customs and traditions of the collective reality. This housemate is like an authority figure who keeps law and order in the house in your head. All the messages you have ever received from your parents, teachers and any authority figure in your imprint years is stored by the Critical Parent, ready to be used against you should you step outside the boundaries of the script designed for you. He sets standards:

"That report is not good enough now, is it?"

"You're rubbish at conversation... so why do you insist on talking?"

"They will never take someone like you seriously."

"Why, oh why, did you wear that old thing today of all days?"

"Listen to yourself, you sound like an idiot."

He sets limits.

"Don't do that again."

"How many times have I told you not to speak to those people?"

He tells you what to do.

"You should have said something... "

"You shouldn't let people treat you like that that."

"Never trust anyone."

"You are a failure if you don't have a house and a big car by the time you're 28 years old. Your father was married by the time he was 24 and it never did him any harm."

"I told you so…"

"You are so stupid, look at the mess you made of things."

"If I were you…"

Everything you do in the collective reality is up for scrutiny and he is your surrogate parent living in your head. He never misses an opportunity to tell you what to do or what not to do. Whatever you do, he is there to reprimand you. With housemates like Critical Parent residing in your head, let me tell you that you do not need enemies. Critical Parent has a symbiotic relationship with the next housemate. Basically he bullies her into submission. Critical Parent talks and Adapted Child listens and complies.

Housemate MR #2 – Adapted Child

Adapted Child, as the name implies, is the housemate that has adapted the most to the indoctrinations of the Big People. She wants so much to fit in. She overthinks everything. She finds it difficult to say "no" and gets herself into all sorts of scrapes and misunderstandings for that reason. She hates conflict and will do anything other than rock the boat. She is compliant and will go along with anything that the housemates want or others impose on her in the collective reality. She has the belief that others are better than her, because they seem to know what they are doing. She believes that she is not very good and so she hates to start stuff more than she hates to finish and let things go. She is the consummate people pleaser. She will go out of her way to please others; often having a martyr-like quality. She can get resentful if people do not recognise her efforts. They seldom do. She is often taken for granted and overlooked. Her constant refrains in life are:

"It doesn't matter."

"Not to worry."

"It was nothing."

"It's only me."

She never misses an opportunity to dismiss herself and her needs. In the collective reality she is passive and invisible.

She is a bag of contradictions. She is constantly out of sorts. The default feeling is 'uncomfortable' but here are some other familiar feelings...

Exposed

"Everyone's looking at me."

Conspicuous

"I feel so awkward."

Ridiculous

"Everyone knows I messed up!"

Stupid

"I have no clue what they are talking about."

Or

"I'm useless."

Anxious

"I'd rather die than deliver the annual presentation to the team."

Guilty

"I feel so guilty that I didn't help Tom with his filing, so that he could go off to play golf."

Nervous

"I hope they don't ask me for my opinion...I will not know what to say."

Lacking in confidence

"I know what I want to say, I just can't say it."

She is the voice in your head that causes you to stress about everything.

The other housemates laugh at her and override her.

Basically, she is bullied. She is always in fear of upsetting the other housemates. She listens to all of them. She second guesses them. She tries to humour them. She tries to keep up. She spends most of her time in her head in your head.

Whenever you go into a situation in the collective reality where you feel unsure or unsafe, Adapted Child shows up. Yet she does you no favours. None whatsoever! She is afraid to speak up, to be seen and to be counted. She is afraid to go for her goals. She is afraid of the housemates. She is afraid of people in the collective reality. She is afraid to live life.

Housemate MR #3 – Little Professor

This next housemate is the Little Professor and he is so called because he is very smart. He hasn't got a university degree in psychology, but he uses his intuition to figure people out. He is the part of you that is intuitive, manipulative and creative. He seems to be able to understand body language to assess a situation long before the other housemates can. He plays hunches to figure things out. He is the part of you that knows when to be quiet, when to cry if necessary and when to give that winning smile. If you use your little professor a lot you have a knack of getting around people.

Little Professor loves to play games. This helps him to stay one step ahead of the other housemates. The games he plays are psychological games. These games have moves just like a game of chess or poker. He never relaxes and there is always a hidden agenda to what he does.

Sometimes he plays big complicated games and sometimes he plays them just for the fun of it.

The games all have the same basic elements:
- The conversation seems innocent.
- The hidden agenda emerges along the way
- The payoff is revealed and Little Professor gets

what he wants without even asking.

Consider this seemingly innocent interaction.

Martha and Arthur are on a training course. As it gets close to the end of the day, Martha starts smiling at Arthur and laughing at his jokes. Casually she asks him:

"Are you going past the station?"

This could be an innocent transaction, but it isn't. What do you think Martha wants…?

Arthur, who has been sucked into Martha's womanly wiles, is confused. He isn't going past the station, but he doesn't want to appear rude. He doesn't want to leave her in the lurch. Nor does he want to appear ungentlemanly.

Without him knowing it, Martha has been manipulating him for the last hour or so to get what she wants which is… a lift to the station.

All Martha has said is, "Are you going past the station?", but with these words Arthur disappears into the worm hole. The whole game is playing out in his head.

Martha's script is: I can get people to do whatever I want.

And

Arthur's script is: Please others.

Games are short scenes in a script. What they do is reinforce the script. Martha, who is an expert manipulator, will not play her game with anyone. She picks up the vibes of those that have the complementary script to her games.

She scents that Arthur's script is one of a guy who needs to please others, and so she wants to help him fulfil his life position of pleasing others by setting things up so that he can do just that.

The Little Professor believes that the world is a dangerous place. He has no option but to attack before being attacked. He will not allow himself to be vulnerable or to be caught out. So he uses games to stop people getting too close to him.

Martha could have asked Arthur for a lift to the station. But in her eyes this would have made her reliant on Arthur and that wouldn't do. So she positions the request as if she doesn't really care what the outcome is.

The Little Professor doesn't believe in open, honest communication.

"In order to form an immaculate member of a flock of sheep one must, above all, be a sheep."

~Chapter Seven~

High Ranking Housemate: Your Ego

One of the high ranking housemates is the Ego. He often gets a bad press, mostly because he is misunderstood. In the collective reality it is said to be bad if you have too big an ego or if you are egotistical. In truth there is nothing wrong with the Ego. His job is to assist you in having your own unique experience of life.

His job is to take information received from your senses and feed it back to the other housemates for them to interpret. He then takes the information from the housemates and feeds it back to the senses and then back into the collective reality. That is the circle of events.

There are about two billion pieces of data coming through your five senses every second. Just imagine if he were to bring every piece of information to your attention, you would go crazy. He does the best he can, the work is endless. The Ego filters the information that you receive into categories. If there is anything that requires attention, it gets a pass and it goes straight to the appropriate housemate who can make the decision. If it is low ranking stuff the low ranking housemates make the decision, and so on. If the information is new and exciting, that can be a source of amusement for the housemates for a while. Everything in the collective reality is filtered. That is to say, the Ego decides if it is worthy of your attention.

He deletes, distorts and generalises information and in so doing gathers a lot of control and power. The housemates rely on what he says and act accordingly. If the information is wrong, the housemates in the virtual reality have no way of correcting it. They can only instruct Ego on the information he has disclosed to them.

Ego is the conduit; normally, he need not do anything

other than pass on information. The problem with Ego is that he is easily bored. On top of that he likes the feeling of power.

The Ego has an ego. He is ego. He is full of his own importance. He is attracted to the finer things in life, because this is food for him. You name it: mobiles, shoes, cars, adventure, he loves it. Sometimes a little too much! It is not important whether you can afford it or not. What Ego wants, Ego gets or he sulks!

"I have to have it... it's so me."

He decides the information and puts his own twist on it because he knows exactly how to keep the other housemates sweet if he wants, or he knows exactly what to say to get them annoyed if he wants.

"You've worked so hard you deserve that new thingummyjig."

Or

"Can you believe what he said ... it is outrageous!"

Or

"If they think I'm going to do that, they can think again."

Or

"Why are you the only one doing the donkey work around here?"

Or

"If they think they can get one over on me they are wrong."

Or

"I'm not apologising to you, for what?"

Or

"Do they know who I am?"

I am reminded here of an amusing story.

A guy of some importance was waiting in a queue to board a flight. There was a delay. He became more and more agitated until finally he couldn't stand it any longer. He marched up to the front desk and demanded to know why there was a delay. The steward tried to tell him the

70

reason but he was having none of it. He angrily said to the steward:

"Do you know who I am?"

The steward, without missing a beat, calmly walked over to the intercom and announced:

"Attention, ladies and gentlemen. I have a man at Check-in number 33 who doesn't know who he is. Please come to the check-in, if you can assist in identifying him. Thank you."

All of the comments that arise from this sort of stimuli from the collective reality are observed by the Ego and then translated to the housemates in the way that Ego wants, in order to incite a response. The housemates react true to form and feed information back to the Ego. It is a system that is sustained by the type of information it filters and doesn't filter.

All the housemates want to be you. If you do not look sharp, they step in to impersonate you. Ego wants to be you more. He intercepts all information in your virtual reality and interrupts information from the collective reality and hands it to you as a deleted, generalised and distorted reality. When you get confused about things that happen to you and around you, he settles the confusion by telling you that you are different from the others. He wants to set you apart from others. He stresses that you are different and misunderstood because he wants to create a sense of separation in you. He needs to do this so that he can divide and rule.

He gives you ideas above your station, so that he can always create a state of tension in you, by telling you that no one understands you or no one will ever be good enough for you. He sets the rules and in order for someone to be worthy of you they need to work in that job, drive that car and command whatever salary. The Ego tells you that because you are so special; you have to eat at a certain place, or go here, there and everywhere for your holidays.

He tells you to visit a country but never see the country. To see things the way they are is not what sustains the Ego.

I was on a world tour many moons ago and travelling with some people who had rampaging egos. One from the party screamed one day in frustration:

"Why don't these damn people speak English?"

We were in Japan. Ego and ignorance is the worst combination ever.

Ego tells you who and who not to talk to.

"Those people are lowlife."

What to wear and what not to wear.

"I wouldn't be seen dead in anything like that."

The standards that the Ego has are unbelievably high for you to achieve.

"I could never shop in that store."

First of all, they are his goals and not wholly yours. He keeps you on the treadmill. He is never satisfied with anything, for him it's all about achieving and never stopping. He is afraid that if he stops and takes a breath you may realise you don't need the latest gadget or 'must have'. The whole idea behind his actions is to keep your self-esteem as low as possible and to elevate him as high as possible. If you are low then surely you would never have the strength or courage to challenge his position. Another distinguishing feature of the ego is that he is never ever wrong.

"Nobody talks to me like that and gets away with it."

"Who do you think you're talking to?"

He sees fighting for something that is blatantly wrong or dumb or petty as a mark of strength.

"It's not the money; it's the principle of the matter."

He gets you to defend things that you don't really know about or care about on a day to day basis, or that don't have any impact on your life.

"That's not right what they are doing in Mongolia."

Ego never allows anyone to get one over on him. Even

if it is life threatening, he sees it as his duty to be the defender of what he deems to be right for you.

I used to have a male friend who used to put our lives in danger every time we went out. I would literally grind my foot into the floor alongside him in the passenger seat, willing him to brake sometimes. If someone drove too fast, too slow, cut him up or whatever, he saw it as a matter of honour to put them right. Many a time we would go tearing off down a street, so that we could catch an unassuming driver up so that he could give them a piece of his mind.

"What's this guy doing... call yourself a driver."

"Come on, love, we haven't got all day."

Ego takes pride in sticking up for what he perceives to be right. The more people don't agree with him the more defiant he becomes. He sticks to his so-called principles.

"You people don't know what you are talking about."

"The fact of the matter is…"

Your Ego loves a good argument, so he can really vent his spleen. He shows up for an argument, even if it is not his argument. He views anything that happens as an opportunity to show superiority. He is more intelligent. He has better taste. The Ego is competitive and so he will not back down, no matter what. He has to have the last word. He will tie himself up in knots trying to figure out how to catch people out or get others back for wrong doings. The Ego bears grudges and will never forgive.

For him, backing down or saying "I'm sorry" is a mark of defeat. This would send signals to the housemates and others in the collective reality that he is not in control. He thinks he is always on stage and that everyone is watching his every move. For that reason he is ridiculous in the collective reality; putting on this false front, getting defensive at the slightest feedback and yet feeling inadequate at the same time.

What is the most frightening thing about the Ego is his mistrust of people and events. He never forgets anything and so often brings wrongdoings from the past into his present day discussions to prove his point.

He is possessive to the point of paranoia. He talks in terms of people as objects and possessions in the same way as he may talk about his dog or car. If anyone tries to encroach on his so-called patch he comes out all guns blazing. He is fragile and super sensitive.

Not so long ago I was returning to my house from a run. It was a beautiful summer's day and so I decided to take the route across the park. People were sitting on the grass in various stages of undress, and enjoying the sun. I don't know what the matter is with English people, but as soon as they glimpse the sun, they take their clothes off!

Anyway, I was cutting across the park when suddenly the calm still day was interrupted by shouting and swearing. I joined the disturbance just when two men were about to come to blows.

Apparently, one guy had looked at another guy's girlfriend for a little too long for his liking. The Looker was subjected to a ton of abuse. I am telling you, just because of his 'three second too long' glance, the boyfriend questioned the Looker's legitimacy and his profession. According to Boyfriend, Looker was an illegitimate pervert.

That is the Ego, right there. Paranoid and possessive. It was such a stupid argument but if common sense hadn't prevailed, I am sure these guys would have ended up rolling around in the grass to protect their honour.

Common sense did prevail. If left up to Ego it would have been pistols at dawn. Boyfriend had everyone in the park's attention. A crowd was gathering. It was battle of the Egos. Boyfriend couldn't back down because girlfriend or potential girlfriend was watching. Boyfriend's Ego would rather have him in hospital than back down in front of the girlfriend. The girlfriend was half-heartedly trying to talk Boyfriend out of it, but her Ego had shown up as well. She was a woman with two men fighting over her.

Wow!

Suddenly the Looker said something like this:

"So what, man, if I look? You have a very attractive girlfriend. I like to admire beauty. Is your ego so fragile that you cannot allow me three seconds?"

Boyfriend was stumped, his Ego not fast enough to retort. I often wonder how long Boyfriend and Girlfriend lasted after that.

Ego uses your information. He takes information from the collective reality and distorts it to suit his purpose. He is fragile, sensitive and easily hurt, because he knows his position in the house is precarious. He is a bag of contradictions. These contradictions are how he keeps you and the other housemates confused. He pretends he is doing everything to protect you but really he is protecting himself. He has no self-esteem and takes every opportunity to steal what little you have. He creates incidents in the collective reality to keep you off the track of discovering that you don't need an Ego.

He is the guy that decided that he should be the leader of the house. He is a jumped up upstart who has taken your position in the house. He is impersonating you.

*"The fear of death is the most unjustified of all fears,
for there's no risk of accident for someone who's dead."*

~Chapter Eight~

High Ranking Housemates: Your Emotions

These housemates rule the roost. Before I go on to
introduce your emotions to you, I want to ask you a
question.

What do you think about ice cream?

Do you like it?

Do you have a favourite flavour?

How do you like it…on its own or with cake or fruit?

Now I have another set of questions for you.

What do you think about your emotions?

Do you like them?

Do you have a recurring emotion?

Do you know how to handle your emotions?

Don't tell me that your answers to the ice cream
questions were more conclusive than the ones about
emotions. Don't worry, you are not alone; most people
don't have a clue about their emotions and how to deal
with them.

The highest ranking of the housemates are your
emotions. Well, let me clarify this; they are in poll position
because there is a bunch of them, and if that wasn't
enough they have lots of friends that just seem to turn up
and hang around for days and months sometimes.

Your emotions are needed for you to interact and
express yourself in the collective reality. Something
happens; you witness it and then feedback the information
to yourself via your emotions. Your emotions alert you to
what is going on out there in the collective reality. If you
had no emotions you wouldn't be able to make any contact
with the collective reality. You may as well be a table for
all the interaction you could have. Your emotions are very
important in so far as they help you engage in your life.

Yet how can you express and fully enjoy what life has to bring if you don't even know how to manage the very tools of expression?

Emotions are your housemates. But because you don't know what to do with them and neither do any of the other housemates for that matter, they run around causing havoc. Everyone in the house tippy toes around them, afraid to get them stirred up. They are like naughty children out of control. They cause you to get heated up, sweaty, shaky, they give you heart palpitations and you hate the feelings they bring. In fact you will do anything other than let your emotions get the better of you. When you go into situations in the collective reality you try with all your might to keep a lid on your emotions. Sometimes it works and sometimes it doesn't. Most of the time it doesn't!

One of the conditions of membership of the collective reality is not to show your emotions. If you see someone having a meltdown in the bank or supermarket, you step aside; who wants to be associated with this person who has lost the plot? If you get too close they may try to reel you in; after all, this emotional malfunction that they have may be contagious. People who are too emotional in the collective reality are showing weakness and their inability to cope.

Your emotions are there to protect you from harm and perceived threat. They are like soldiers, they don't ask questions. They spring into action to protect you and serve you at the slightest provocation. They do not care whether the threat is real or not, small or great, past, present or future, near or far. The focus is always the same. Fight like mad or run like crazy. They have been allowed to rule the roost for so long, now they are powerful and out of control.

These energy stealers have connections in high places and it is this that gives them ideas above their station. They have connections to your hardware: the brain. The amygdala is the control to your anger and fear and the centre in the brain from where these housemates take their instructions. The hypothalamus reads the environment and sends information to the brain for processing. If the environment is perceived as hostile, the information is picked up by the amygdala. The amygdala then bombards the body with adrenalin and hormones. Your body has no choice but to fall in line. Your heart starts racing as you prepare to fight or take flight, and you feel that you are going to have a heart attack. You start to breathe heavily or you can't catch your breath. Your mouth is dry and you find it difficult to swallow. Your limbs start shaking and you feel as if you are losing control over them. Your stomach churns and you feel that you are about to empty the contents of your bowels. Your knees feel weak and your sphincter twitches. You find it difficult to express yourself, you cannot concentrate and you feel you are losing your mind.

All of this happens because you are preparing to respond to an emergency. The body increases your sugar levels so that you can only focus on the threat at hand. These guys steal your ability to think straight and because of what they do to your body, they steal your energy too. After you have gone through a fight with your emotions, you feel exhausted.

Let's focus on the emotion called 'Fear' for a moment. He is one of the gang leaders. He is there to protect you from danger. Most people love to slate him as the bad guy.

"You have to conquer your fears," they say.

Actually, he is a good guy. All your emotions are. They are there to serve a purpose and that purpose is you. Imagine how long you would last in the African jungle without fear. Fear tells you to watch out. Anger may give you the aggression you need to hunt food. Hope may give you the motivation to continue. If you are confronted by a lion you are going to need every emotion you can muster to get out of that situation, or at least put up a good fight.

The housemate Fear has ideas above his station,

because he thinks he needs to jumps in when you don't particularly need him; giving a presentation at work, when you want to travel, change your job, or do something new, form a new relationship. He is not required but he shows up anyway. I have a fear of snakes. I don't know why. I have never even seen a snake apart from behind the glass in a zoo. If I even think of a snake my body starts to shake, shudder and a cold sweat descends. How about you? What's your irrational fear?

For you it may be public speaking or getting people to take you seriously. There are two types of Fears: physiological and psychological.

Let me explain what I mean by this. You and I, as a species, we have not evolved physiologically since our caveman times. We still walk upright; we still eat with our mouths and breathe through our noses. You get the drift. But what have you taken on board psychologically over the last thousands of years? Wow! You can barely adjust to one change when you are overtaken by another. Fear does not like change. Every time you are presented with a new thing, fear does a back flip. He talks to the brain, the brain releases the drugs and you become a nervous wreck.

Fear of stuff that you *should* be afraid of is OK. Who is going to argue about being afraid of a shark or a bear? So Fear deals with physical threats very well indeed. The fundamental difference between Fear factor one: the physiological and Fear factor two: the psychological, is this. In Fear factor one you rely on the efficiency of your brain to decide if and how dangerous the threat is. You manage and control the Fear. In Fear factor two the Fear cannot see the actual danger; it imagines danger and becomes very twitchy and acts on your behalf.

When did Fear start to play such a major role in the house? And who gave him permission to have a fricking opinion on just about anything you do or even think about doing?

As I say, in your imprint stage you were bombarded

with Fear tactics.

"Eat this or you will not be strong."

"Do this or you will never amount to anything."

"Wear this, otherwise you will catch cold."

"Don't talk to those people. They are not to be trusted, they are not like us."

You learn very quickly that the world is a dangerous place. The stories about dungeons and dragons, witches and monsters are true. You learn to be afraid, very afraid. It starts very early in your life, when you were not sophisticated enough to figure out fact from fiction and, more to the point, when you cannot tell the people around you, the 'Fear bringers', to leave you alone.

Fear, the fastest of all the emotions, latches on to you and becomes your new best friend and works his way into you. He finds out your weak spots and what will keep you and he bonded forever. In your formative years when you barely had a handle on what was going on in your life, you had to learn so much. Fear steps in to become your parent. Fear is your protective parent at home, at school, at work and your protector against the world.

In your imprint stage everything is confusing. If you had emotional intelligence at this point in your life you would have been able to direct your emotions as they surfaced. You would have been able to tell them when and where and to what degree you needed them. You did not have emotional intelligence so when things happened to you in the collective reality you felt confused as to how to react.

You say:

"Why is this happening to me?"

"What did I do wrong?"

"Why is it not happening to others?"

"What is wrong with me?"

You decide:

"If there is something wrong with me then I had better hide so that no one ever finds out."

Someone has to take charge and save you.

The battlefields...

Father (angrily); "Get out of my sight... "
Mother: "I swear I don't know where he gets it from."
(Ridicule)
Fear: "I'll protect you from this foolish family." The
antidote *Hide your feelings.*

Or

Classmate (threatening): "I am going to beat you up after
school."
You: "Why?"
Classmate: "I just don't like you. You make me sick...
you're fat/ugly." (Humiliating)
Fear: "I'll protect you from this fool." The antidote: *Don't
give eye contact and pretend you are invisible.*

Or

Teacher (condescending): "Yes! Jo, you know that you
know but give others a chance to answer."
Jo: "But I know the answer, Miss."
Teacher: "It is not polite to draw attention to yourself in
this manner. Nobody likes a Show off!" (Humiliation)
Everyone laughs.
Fear: "I'll protect you from this foolish system." The
antidote: *Never speak up in a group again, ever.*

Or

Teacher (suspicious): "You have done well in the maths
test, did anyone help you with the answers?"
Peers: "Cheat. Nerd!" (Ridicule)
Fear: "I'll protect you from this foolish situation." The
antidote: *Learn to dumb down."*

Or

You: "I want to start a band."
Uncle (laughing mockingly): "People like us don't start
bands; we are the ones that go to watch the band. It's
better you know your place so that nothing bad can happen

to you."

You: "Like what?"

Uncle: "What happens if you meet a bad manager or a bad woman or you lose your money or you have an accident on the road or a piece of the stage falls and breaks your neck or a deranged fan throws acid in your face?"

Fear: "I'll protect you from everything." The antidote: *Don't go for your dreams.*

Or

Mother: "Don't think that way; people will think you are crazy."

Fear: "I'll protect you from those foolish people." The antidote: *Don't think, don't be creative and do not think outside of the box.*

Or

You: "Can I play with you?"

Them: "No, no one likes you…you're boring."

Fear: "I'll protect you from everyone." The antidote: *Do not get close to people; they will only hurt you in the end.*

Fear does his job. Whatever you are afraid of; Fear will fix it for you. He will use himself to protect you. Fear is afraid of everything and you need to be too.

What has happened here is that you have formed a relationship with Fear.

Fear hates the feeling of being afraid. How can sweaty armpits be pleasant to anyone? Fear prefers it when you keep very still. No sudden moves. No sudden desires to venture out or change. Fear promised to protect you from all harm. But you want to do stuff. Go for this job. Travel… and why not? He has to keep you in check. He has to keep you from all harm. When I say all harm I mean all harm. That is present and future, real or perceived. Doesn't matter the intensity, the impact on your life or whether it is going to help you realise your potential. He does his job so well that you are stuffed.

Fear never travels alone... that's too scary. He always

brings reinforcements. Fear uses his housemates Perfection, Doubt, Guilt, Panic and Anger. He uses all these housemates to bring another flavour to the proceedings, to mix it up a bit and throw you of off his scent.

Fear said he would protect you from pain. But he didn't give you the fine details of the contract. You didn't know that whilst you were signing the deeds to prevent a particular pain situation happening again, that the small print stated that you had signed over your whole emotional intelligence to him as well.

Let's talk about pain for a moment. At the first pain event, your brain talked to your amygdala and the amygdala fired off cortisol and adrenalin, to name but two, at the problem. Fear was released. The big problem started when Fear decided that he liked his freedom and moreover he liked the power and control he had over you. He could make you shiver. He could make you sweat. In some instances he could actually make you forget your own name. Such power! He decided that he was going to make you fearful of just about everything and everyone, so that you would have to defer to him for everything. Everything has to be run past Fear to see if it is OK with him to proceed. Usually the answer is "no", as he makes you feel so bad about doing anything you decide it is not worth the hassle. You observe your life slipping away. Opportunities come and go. You become a 'coulda shoulda' person. You, instead of living the dream, are having a near-life experience. He mocks your audacity for thinking that you could do things or make a difference to your life. He attacks your self-esteem, using his 'best friend' self-loathing. He challenges your every move. He beats you down; every phrase from him starts with:

"What if this happens? What about that?"

Your psychic energy is spent on stress and strife thinking and second guessing. He chastises you and scolds you and yet he proclaims to protect you. "It's for your own good," he says. He tells you to know your place, to not step out of line or he will leave you and then what would happen to you?

Here are a few of Fear's chums. I present them in no particular order. Fear asks them to watch over you, depending on the situation that you face. He utilises the right one at the right time with the right degree of intensity so as to keep you locked in your position, until you give up all ideas of escape. He enlists his chums just in case he misses something and you get away. He uses guerrilla warfare and tactics.

Self-loathing pokes you. Self-loathing is an *extreme* self-esteem issue. Self-loathing can lead to you becoming self-defeating or self-sabotaging, where your disregard for yourself leads you to mess up your own plans and actions, thus reinforcing your own negative self-image, and so the circle goes around.

You may say to me that this all a bit extreme, yet how many times have you talked yourself out of something you know in your heart that you could do if you put your mind to it? You see people with half the smartness you have succeeding and enjoying their fruits... and for you it's all a struggle.

The emotional detachment you experience resulting from this combination of low self-esteem and negative world-view can affect your willingness to recognise and go easy on yourself. In fact, it becomes a hobby where you constantly beat yourself up. Over time, you get so accustomed to experiencing the negative feelings that accompany low self-esteem or self-loathing, that you feel worthless and unimportant. You give up.

Your sense of self is formed (in large part) by the way you were treated in the imprint stage. As a child you made judgments about the way you were treated, and you made judgements as to whether that treatment was wrong or right. How you did this was to look at others to see if they were getting the same treatment as you.

"Why did this happen to me?"

Or

"Why did they hurt me?"

When faced with a stressful situation of any nature, you had your sense of right and wrong, fair or unfair, violated. This was very confusing to you, especially as the people doing the injustice were family and friends. In order to make sense of what was happening to you, you made a crucial decision. A decision in your imprint years, when you didn't have all the facts, that influences how you live your life today.

"There is something wrong with me."

"I am not good enough."

"I am not worthy."

"Other people are better than me."

This decision is precisely what causes low self-esteem, lack of confidence and a stressful existence.

When your feelings and needs are consistently invalidated, when you are repeatedly hurt by people whom you love and trust and who are supposed to love you too, judgments about who is good and who is bad become very confused within you. You may notice that others in your circle, such as peers or siblings, are not ridiculed and rejected while you are, then you say to yourself people are good or right, and I am bad or wrong.

Once you accept this faulty value judgment, you evaluate the situation from the vantage point that Fear has created for you. You conclude:

"I deserve this."

"It must be my fault."

Your confusion is pointed inwards and you internalise your emotions rather than express them.

The moral part of the self, discerning right from wrong, blames the self for the problems you are having and the unpleasant feelings that result. Fear jumps in to save you from everything that he himself has created for you, professing to be on your side. He assures you that he will protect you from the shame of not living up to everyone else's expectations of you and what you should be. You feel that you have failed in the fundaments of life and your only friend is Fear.

Perfectionism is another one of Fear's chums. At first glance perfectionism can appear unassuming. High-achieving individuals such as athletes, scientists, and artists possess the right mix of motivation, skill and perfectionism to achieve their goals. They recognise that perfection is a journey and they use it to push themselves further along the path of success.

The perfectionism that is meted out by Fear is a pathological issue which can become detrimental to your everyday life. For example, if you have an intense desire to be perfect you may find yourself procrastinating because you are unable to start and complete a task perfectly. "I'm a perfectionist," you may say, even convincing yourself that this is something to be proud of. It is used today as a badge of honour. It is delusionary and destructive. It stops you from starting anything; it prevents you from sticking at anything without getting disenchanted. It stops you from getting close to anyone, ever. Because when a relationship doesn't go according to plan, you get to wave the get out of jail card called 'perfection'.

"The relationship wasn't perfect."

"The opportunity wasn't perfect."

"The timing wasn't perfect."

It's black or white, either/ or, all or nothing! Nothing is ever perfect. Why? Because nothing is. This is the bind that has you trapped. Fear, using perfection as his double-edged sword, persuades you that nothing is worth the effort because nothing is good enough. He tells you to stay hidden until there is a perfect situation or person to come out for. As perfection doesn't exist, you are going to be there in your hidey hole for a very long time.

Anxiety is good friends with Fear. He is an ally that

keeps Fear informed if the going gets too tough. You get stressed and anxious at work, at home, in traffic and about life, of course you do. But sometimes Anxiety comes a-calling and he doesn't want to leave. He sticks around and he becomes too big and hard to manage and won't go away; it becomes a disabling disorder. Anxiety increases to a level that affects your ability to participate in everyday life and your ability cope or engage in your own life. Anxiety makes you take a back seat in your life and hand over the driving to someone, anyone. I don't know which is worst; to hand over the driving to someone or to just abdicate and career out of control, driverless.

If Anxiety cannot grab your attention then he will call for reinforcement. This heavy is called Depression. It is a powerful sensation that sweeps all over your body, mind and mood. It is a fog that affects your eating, sleeping, the way you view the collective reality and the way you think about yourself in the collective reality.

Depression is the result of blocked feelings taking hold of you. Depression suggests to you that there is no way out of your situation. And instead of helping you to find a way out, Depression causes you to turn in on yourself and against yourself. Depression feeds on you, taking away any fight you may have left in reserve. Of course Fear and chums love this situation. Because then you are too weak to resist the onslaught. You can't be bothered to try too much, as you know that all roads lead to failure, hurt and despair.

So you now know that Fear has many emotional chums that he can call on to hold you in place. You name it and he can conjure up your biggest insecurities. In fact, he has so much intelligence on you that he knows what your insecurities are even before you do. He plays cruel games with you by lulling you into feeling that you can do something; he smiles as you hope for a green light and then laughs in your face when he smashes on the brakes.

He is the gang leader and he works on you with all his

chums. Fear proves to you time and time and time again that you can't achieve anything and so your self-esteem disappears down the rabbit hole, and he has you just where he wants you.

Over time and after years of trying to succeed at anything and with anyone, you give up all rights to your life. It is at this point that Fear can leave you alone for long periods of time. He knows that you will not make a bid for freedom. He knows you will not do anything rash. Because he has built up so much self-doubt, mistrust of yourself and others, such lack of confidence in your own abilities that you dare not even think of trying. Trust no one, believe in no one. Be on red alert for attack.

They say that when you get burned by fire you don't put your hand in the hot oven again. But that's not necessarily the case. Sometimes, it's the fact of being burned that emotionally bonds you to an abuser. In fact, studies show that emotional abuse intermixed with small acts of kindness can bond some victims to their abusers even more than consistent good treatment can. I am saying here that your abuser is your own fear.

The Stockholm Syndrome

I want to talk about a phenomenon that exists called the Stockholm Syndrome. You may think this is not you, this is too extreme. That may be the case but it is all a matter of degree. If you are afraid of life then chances are you are suffering from Stockholm Syndrome in some form or fashion.

Stockholm Syndrome (also known as 'terror bonding' and 'traumatic bonding') is a paradoxical and psychological phenomenon in which hostages feel empathy and positive feelings toward their captors – sometimes, even defending them. Over time, a hostage victim may come to believe that the abuse he or she has endured was out of kindness or love on the part of the captor.

These feelings may appear to be irrational by others, as the hostage had endured much danger and risk during his or her captivity.

Approximately one quarter of all hostage victims display Stockholm Syndrome after a period of captivity.

Stockholm Syndrome is a form of traumatic bonding, in which strong emotional ties develop between two people when one person intermittently beats, harasses, abuses or intimidates the other person.

Stockholm Syndrome is not the subject of ridicule – it can happen to anyone – it is the ultimate in survival mechanisms.

The precise reason that some people develop Stockholm Syndrome while others do not is complex.

People who develop Stockholm Syndrome have come to identify with (and possibly care about) their captors in an unconscious and desperate act of self-preservation. Stockholm Syndrome most frequently develops during traumatic situations like kidnapping, domestic abuse, or hostage situations, and the effect of this disorder doesn't necessarily stop once the victim has been released.

Most victims who have Stockholm Syndrome continue to care for and defend their captors long after they've escaped captivity.

Why?

Self-preservation is the answer.

A hostage feels as though his or her captor is doing him or her a favour by allowing them to remain alive. Many prisoners are treated in a sympathetic manner by their captors, allowing them to see their captors in a positive manner. After all, aren't captors supposed to be cruel?

Isolation from the outside world allows the hostage to see the world through the eyes of the captor – the prisoner begins to empathise and sympathise with his or her captor. It is soon the only world the prisoner knows. The captor and prisoner may even begin to share common interests after being together a while.

The prisoner develops a dependence upon his or her abductor – after all, the captor has allowed the prisoner to live, even treated them kindly (in most cases, the kindness is merely perceived).

While most people associate Stockholm Syndrome with a captor/prisoner relationship, any number of people may develop it, including physically and emotionally abused children, people in dysfunctional relationships and prisoners of war.

Let's have a look at where this phenomenon originated.

Back in 1972, two men entered a bank in Stockholm, Sweden, intending to rob it. The police were called, and when they burst into the bank, the two robbers shot them, thus beginning a hostage situation.

For six long days, these robbers held four people who had been in the bank hostage, at gunpoint, sometimes strapping explosives on them, at other times putting nooses around their necks.

By the time the police were able to attempt to rescue, the hostages fought the police off in defence of their captors, blaming the situation entirely upon the police. One of the hostages, once free, set up a fund to cover his captor's legal fees.

The term 'Stockholm Syndrome' was born, finally capturing the bizarre essence of the captor/prisoner phenomenon; in your case, you and Fear.

The features of Stockholm Syndrome include some of the following:

- Positive feelings from the prisoner toward the captor.
- Negative feelings from the prisoner toward his or her family, friends or authorities attempting any support.
- Support for the captor's reasons and behaviours.
- Positive feelings on the part of the captor toward the victim.

- Support from the victim to help the captor.
- Inability by the victim to execute behaviours that could lead to release or detachment from the captor.

In order for Stockholm Syndrome to occur, there must be at least three of the following traits:

- There must be a sorely uneven balance of power in which the captor must dictate what the captive can and cannot do.
- There must be the threat of death or physical injury to the captive from the captor.
- There must be a self-preservation instinct within the prisoner.
- The prisoner believes (perhaps falsely) that he or she cannot escape.
- Survival is dependent upon following the rules of the captor.
- The prisoner must be isolated from others who are not being held captive.

It does happen. Here's how...

1) After a very emotionally traumatic and stressful situation, a person finds his or herself held captive by a captor who threatens to kill or hurt them if they do not follow the rules. Abuse – physical or emotional or both– occurs. The prisoner has difficulty thinking straight – escape is not an option, right? If they try to escape, something awful may happen.

The prisoner believes that the only way for everyone to survive is to be obedient to the captor.

2) Time marches on. The captor is under stress, and becomes more demanding and erratic. The fluctuating moods of the captor lead to unexpected violence and abuse. The prisoner then learns what triggers may or may not set off their captor as a means of survival.

This, however, means that *the prisoner learns more*

about his or her captor.

3) The prisoner begins to see the captor as being kind. Sometimes you may be allowed to try new things, go for a new job even travel abroad. In this way, the captor plays good cop/bad cop.

The slightest act of kindness feels like a sign of friendship that the prisoner clings to.

4) Over time, the captor begins to appear less and less threatening and more of a means of survival than harm. In order to survive psychologically and to ease the crisis situation of their life, the prisoner begins to believe that the captor is actually a friend, that he will not kill them, and that they can work together to get out of the mess they're in. Rather than see the people on the outside trying to rescue the prisoner as the saviours, instead, they appear to be enemies – they will hurt the captor, who is now his or her 'friend' and 'protector.'

The captor has gone from 'captor' to 'friend' in a process of self-delusion and self-preservation on the part of the prisoner.

5) This bonding leads to incredibly conflicted feelings within the prisoner or abuser. The victim may begin to feel concern for the captor; at times, ignoring his or her own needs.

The victim is conflicted about his or her feelings toward the captor.

6) When the traumatic event is over, the victim can undergo an incredibly hard transition.

The emotional shackles of Stockholm Syndrome can last a lifetime.

Do you see any of yourself in the description of Stockholm Syndrome?

So why do you continue to be at the beck and call of Fear; when did he turn things around so that he stopped working for you and you found yourself on *his* payroll? What are the main factors why you stay in this dysfunctional relationship? Why has Fear developed such psychopathic tendencies of beating you up for trying and then soothing the pain when you fail? Where did Fear develop such narcissistic tendencies where he turns every occasion to be all about him?

Who or what drives Fear? Is there any emotion more powerful? Is there a dark lord to whom even Fear must bow? Of course there is. He is the 'uber' housemate. His name is Shame. Shame is the final frontier.

"Whoever undertakes to set himself up as a judge of Truth and Knowledge is shipwrecked by the laughter of the gods."

~Chapter Nine~

Highest Ranking Housemate Of All: Shame

Let's talk about shame.

Being ashamed is as close to death as you can get.

"I nearly died of shame."

You don't want to get it wrong, say the wrong thing or do the wrong thing. You have to be right. If you dare to be anything less than perfect, Shame will unleash her sharp tentacles of humiliation, exposure, embarrassment and damn foolishness. Antidote: do nothing and say nothing.

You can't even trip over in the street. What would others think of me? There should be no room for failure. Antidote: Do nothing and go nowhere. You cannot afford to make a fool of yourself over something or worse, somebody. Attachment or intimacy or belonging is not good for the soul. Vulnerability is a messy thing. It is stark and coal facing. It is one of those words which is right up there with shame and can cause grown people to flinch. Antidote: do not get close to people. Only go so far and then run for the hills. Shame is the arch enemy within. You will do anything not to feel its cold clammy breath on the back of your neck, whispering how ridiculous you are and its stifling paralyzing embrace rendering you into submission. The moment of feeling ashamed is like having an 'out of body experience', but not in a good way. It is like being taken over by something.

There is actually a physical feeling of opening up. Whoosh! You feel cold, clammy breeze under your armpits and your genitalia. Feelings of shame are familiar. You know them. You know what to expect and you know the consequences. You do not want to go into that pain again. You know that if you go into that space all your demons are

94

sitting there waiting for you. You are the guest of honour. All the reinforced feelings of your inadequacies are there, sitting at the table waiting to greet you, to talk about old times: culture, family, peers, your job and your appearance. In that room you are confronted with stark conclusions you made years ago about your situation.

What did you decide?

"They don't like me."

"They don't love me."

"They don't accept me."

"They don't want me".

The exposure to that knowledge hurts like hell. Every time you do something such as speaking up or getting close to something or someone, trying something different, putting yourself on the line, that is what you hear ringing in your ears. That is what you hear. That is what you feel. Those sensations are like going up to the highest peak on a mountain and looking over.

The sensation of falling or losing your footing is terrifying. The presumed fear of anything sends you off, intentionally barking up the wrong tree. You do stuff, achieve stuff and it still doesn't quell the dread you feel inside when trying to do life. Fear is the disguise sent by Shame to confuse you. While you are so busy trying to confront, combat and reframe Fear, Shame is the real deal...and she, the emotion who must be obeyed, is left to go wreak hazard on your life's potential. Other emotions come and go; you feel sad today, tomorrow not so sad and the next day better. Shame, on the other hand, is an emotion that never goes away. Not easily anyway. You can't shake it off with a "oh well here I go again". The feelings of ridiculousness and humiliation have a lot of staying power.

So instead you tiptoe around, afraid to wake the 'bugger' up. What example can I give you? Let's say back at school a so-called friend let it be known to everyone that you liked a certain boy in your class. You would have to live with the shame of being in his presence every day. Living the shame that he knows and so does everyone else. You walk the walk of shame every day.

Not so long ago I was walking down my local high street, minding my own business, when suddenly, I found myself sprawled out on the ground. For no apparent reason (there was no banana skin) I just lost control of my feet and I fell over them. Well, I was on the ground for about five seconds, I picked myself up so fast a middle-weight boxing champion would have been proud. I looked up and down the street to see if anyone had noticed or more to the point, if anyone was laughing. No one was. Then Shame hit me.

"What's wrong with you?"

"Can't you even walk now?"

"Everyone is looking at you."

"All dressed up and you can't even put one foot in front of the other."

"Imagine if that had happened at work."

Let me tell you that since that day I have never walked along the high street without thinking about my tumble. I know where I fell. I know the time of day and I know what I was wearing! I have never worn that particular pair of shoes again. It is going to take me a while to live that one down. You see I didn't and I still don't have a fear of falling over; it was the shame of falling that got me!

Shame bites at the conditions for your healthy existence in the collective reality.

There are three conditions required in life for you to feel emotionally healthy. They are:

1. To feel significant and that you matter.

2. To feel intimate and close to another.

3. To feel that you are able to achieve your goals.

If you cannot succeed in these three, then you feel Shame.

It is tantamount to getting a loudspeaker and telling everyone that you are getting it wrong and that you are a living, breathing, walking, talking joke!

1. *The shame of Insignificance*

One of the biggest shames of a person is the knowledge that they were born and raised and will die and are of no consequence. You couldn't figure out the code of life. You came, you saw and it meant bugger all. You failed and there is big shame in that for you. The whole essence of our being human calls out for meaning. You need to know the point but more than that you need to know that you have a point. Having a point is different from having a point of view. That's not what I am talking about. I am talking about purpose. The fact that you don't think that your life makes any sense means that you were made to feel worthless and invisible. Someone did a number on you and their intention was to rub you out. To make you not exist. Someone or something erased your point. There's shame for you in the fact that you let it happen in the first place. There is shame for you because it continues to be your experience. There is shame because you still can't crack the code. You do not even know how to play the game of life that other lesser beings seem to be able to do with ease. It isn't the fear of living that stumps you; it is the shame of living and not making a difference.

2. *Shame of intimacy*

Intimacy is a big one. It probably is the one that got you into the mess in the first place. You presumed affection where there was little or none. You opened your heart expecting love and someone significant gave you indifference in return.

Let's say someone breaks through your armour of 'pretending not to care'. They even seem to enjoy your company and your obtuse way of looking at things. They laugh at your jokes. You want to tell them they are important too and so they should stick around.

You may even want to tell someone you love them. Fear stabs you hard in the belly, so hard that you have to run to the bathroom.

"Don't be so stupid, how could anyone love *you?*"

It is not a defining romantic moment to have a twitchy sphincter. Every time you make a stab at intimacy, your backside starts playing up. Fear warns you to back off. Perfection is one of his friends. He enlists him on a mission to go get you back and encourages you to find fault and finish the relationship.

So now just the way they talk, which used to delight you, is now the source of extreme irritation. You imagine all sorts of things but mostly you imagine them getting too close. They want to make decisions on your behalf. They speak about your future as if you have no say in the matter. It can get to the point where you need to break away because you can feel their breath on your back at night and it is claustrophobic. You imagine that they are spying on you to get even closer, to get data on you so that you surrender to them. Perfection will find fault. "It's too soon." "It's not long enough." "They don't understand me." "He is stifling me." "I can't relate to this." "I can't relate to that." "They have no future." "I need my space."

It is only a matter of time. There will be something wrong. When perfection finds it, Fear welcomes you back with open arms. He plays good cop/ bad cop with you.

The shame of intimacy is because you cannot bear to be seen. To be exposed. For someone to take a good look at you and declare that they don't like what they see. The very thought of getting hurt again would be excruciating. You were open once and you got pissed on from a great height. You vowed that you would never allow anyone to get close enough to hurt you again. In fact, you would never allow yourself to get excited about anything for too long…just in case. The better bet is to keep moving. If the relationship gets complicated or demanding in any way, then you will invent complications. If the relationship goes on for too long, you will invent boredom. The most important thing is that you need to be the one to call the shots. You, at all times, need to be one step ahead so that you can call it a day if there is a danger of getting caught. No, Siree, you are not putting your hand in that cookie jar again! It is not the fear of loving another that you fear, it is the shame of loving and being made a fool of that you fear the most.

3. *Shame of failure*

As you look around in the Hall of Shame, you notice now that Fear is just a foot soldier. Fear is a 'gopher'. Fear protects you from whatever is out there in the collective reality so that you don't get to experience the eternal feeling of shame of not succeeding. Fear is as afraid of it just as much as you are. It is the shame of failing, not the fear of failure that you run from.

There are many courses and classes out there about 'confronting your fears' or feeling the fear and doing stuff anyway. You may have been on several of them yourself. They say that the more you do, the less Fear will have a hold on you. That is true to a point. But it doesn't hit the spot.

"Confront your fears" or "fear is not an option."

People do confront their fears, and that is why you have extreme sport.

There is someone as we speak hauling themselves out of an airplane just to prove to themselves that they can do anything that they put their mind to. What is proves is that they can jump out of an airplane and not much more, because as soon as they touch the ground, Fear is going to grip them by the posterior again. Jumping out of an airplane is not the issue... oh, if only it was as simple as that! It isn't. Fear and Shame will be back. It isn't the fear of failing that you fear. People do stuff and fail all the time. It is the shame of doing things and people finding out that you messed up.

You see, Fear is a disguise sent by Shame to confuse us. They are bedroom buddies. While you are so busy trying to confront, combat, go through the fear, step outside your comfort zone or reframe Fear, Shame is directing the traffic of emotions. Oh, she's good.

Most of us get it that we are going to die at some point. And most of us can intellectualise about that fact. You hear platitudes all the time.

"Live life to the full because you are a long time dead." Or

"Life is short."

So death is not the issue.

In a survey conducted in the USA, it is reported that many people would prefer to die than face their fears. So you would rather die than face your fears? What keeps you paralysed like a rabbit in the headlights of your life? The feeling of Shame is like dying, not like being dead. It is like going through the process of dying. It is like being witness to your own death while still being alive. It is like waking up and living through the death throes every day. You become the living dead. You know and you suspect that everyone else does too. You imagine that everyone is talking about you. "There goes such and such... he tried but he failed... what a shame…"

Shame is like having cancer of the emotions.

Everyone knows someone that has succumbed to cancer. Everyone is terrified of getting it, because the dying is excruciating to watch. No one wants to talk about it, for fear that if you say its name you will anger it and unleash its wrath. That is what Shame's hold on you is like.

"Weakness of attitude becomes weakness of character."

~Chapter Ten~

The Housemates' Assistants: The Behaviours

There are two housemates who live in the house as assistants to the housemates. You know, like the live-in help. They work for particular housemates and provide the behaviors that reflect them in the collective reality. So the housemates tell you what to think and the assistants carry out their bidding in the collective reality. The assistants' feedback information to the housemates and so it goes around and around.

These assistants are Passive and Aggressive. They are called the Behaviours. The Behaviours are natural insofar as they are instinctive and are linked to your primal response to danger, which is fight or flight. These behaviour patterns helped when your ancestors lived in caves. Those instinctive responses were key to their survival. Now, you do not live in a cave. There are no sabre-toothed tigers around. You do not have to go out and catch your dinner. That age has gone. Yet the housemates endorse and perpetuate these behaviours in you so they can control you and predict the outcome of your actions. You oscillate between fighting and fleeing. You think you have no other alternative. Like the Lady Gaga song, you tell yourself you were 'born this way'. It causes them great amusement when you 'lose it' in the collective reality. Because they know that you will retreat to lick your wounds. When an entity is wounded it is weak and vulnerable. It can listen to instructions without resistance.

Let's examine the two Behaviours.

Aggressive Behaviour

When you act aggressively you are acting out the wishes

of your housemates: Critical Parent, Ego, Emotions, and Free Child.

"It shouldn't be allowed," they tell you. They say: "Do something." They poke you.

"Are you going to let them get away with that? Say something," they egg you on.

"Don't let him talk to you like that. Your father would never stand for that behaviour." They taunt you.

They talk to you nonstop in your head.

"You are such a pussy."

In order to satisfy all of them you have to come out all guns blazing. When you are being aggressive, chances are you are overreacting. Why? Because the housemates have to remind you of past ills and wrongs to get you fired up. They tell you that now is your chance to get back at the world.

"Remember that teacher that spoke to you in a similar manner?"

"Remember that guy on holiday once in 2004 that treated you badly? Now is your chance."

They stop you from working in the here and now, which would make them redundant. The way they perpetuate aggressive behaviour in you is to tell you that others are less intelligent than you and therefore deserve what they get from you. They have to give you this superiority complex to mask the fact that you have no self-esteem and very little confidence to conduct yourself in a manner appropriate to the situation.

You are being aggressive when you impose your will on another person.

"You're mad for going to the gym."

You are being aggressive when you threaten someone.

"Do it or you'll lose your job."

You are aggressive when you say negative things.

"This relationship is going nowhere."

You are being aggressive when you're being sarcastic.

"Don't worry about me; I'll just clean the house... again!"

You are being aggressive when you treat anyone less than equal.

"You stupid moron, can't you see the traffic?"

You are being aggressive when you do not listen.

"I don't care what they say…no one can tell me what to do."

The housemates tell you that the only way to redress the imbalance of justice is for you to fight back. It is the *Hunger Games* and you have to show that you are eligible to survive. No one is safe; the person who takes three seconds too long to get started at the traffic lights; the old lady that forgets her kitty litter in the supermarket; the company that kept you waiting on the phone for 7.5 minutes and plays Beatles' songs. It shouldn't be allowed! They are all doing it to you. You should take it very personally!

When you think of someone being aggressive we tend to think of someone in a rage and steam coming out of their ears. But on a day to day basis you are more likely to encounter indirect aggressive behaviour or manipulation. This behaviour is the work of the Little Professor housemate.

Remember, he is the housemate who is very smart and he encourages you to play games with people so that he can prove to himself how smart he is. He uses you to do this.

You do the work of the Little Professor when you are not being open and honest with yourself and others. Instead, you play games. Now, games come in all shapes and sizes. They come in varying degrees of intensity and impact on your life.

There are games where you manipulate others and there are games where you are the one being manipulated.

"If you loved me, you would buy me flowers."

All games are played to confirm your script. I have a friend who has wanted to lose weight for over 25 years now. Think about it; why would someone who desperately wants to lose weight, never lose weight? Why would they sabotage themselves at every juncture? That is because she has a 'don't succeed' script.

"I just have to see cake and I put on weight…"

"I eat when I'm bored."

"I eat when I am stressed."

"I eat when I'm upset."

"I'm big boned."

"I was invited to this party and there was food."

"If I don't eat on time I feel faint."

"I hate exercising."

Another friend drinks like a fish; why would he do that when he knows what the alcohol is doing to his health? Why, because he has a 'don't exist' script.

"I need to drown my sorrows."

"I escape from my problems in the bottle."

"I drink to forget."

Why would someone walk away from a relationship even though they know there was nothing wrong with it? Why? Because they have a 'don't be close' script.

"It's not you… it's me."

"I just need my space."

You have two choices with your script. You either act it out every day. Or you change it. But until that day, chances are you are part of the games that reinforce your play. Even the bit players on the fringe of your life support your script.

You manipulate someone every time you are not straight with them and the only reason why you are not straight is your fear of rejection, being vulnerable or even ridiculed. Playing games takes an enormous amount of energy; there you are playing games with people who are actually playing games with you. They are specialists in their games and you are an expert in yours. Their only way to succeed is to be even more devious and convoluting. Where does that lead you?

Passive Behaviour

Passivity is another of your behaviours. When you are acting passively you are listening to and acting out the instructions of Adapted Child, Identity, Nurturing Parent and Cognitive Dissonance. Passivity is basically giving your power away to others. You allow people to make decisions that affect your life on a daily basis.

"You decide."

"It's up to you."

 You let people get away with it by telling yourself:

"It doesn't matter."

You underrate your abilities:

"I'm only an assistant."

You dismiss yourself.

"It's only me..."

You place other people's wishes above your own... all the time!

"I suppose it's OK if you want me to work late. I'll have to miss my doctor's appointment that I have had booked for a month, but if you want me to stay, I'll do it."

You allow yourself to be treated badly.

"Jen doesn't mind if I give her all the donkey work to do... do you Jen?"

You don't take yourself seriously.

"I'm terribly sorry... I just wanted to say something. It doesn't matter now."

The housemates in question advise you that the best way to survive is to dumb down, act stupid and do whatever it takes not to draw attention to yourself. When you are passive you are overly concerned with what people think. You have a desire to please others. It's like a disease. You hate confrontation and conflict. You would rather chop off your right arm than rock the boat. People quickly pick up the fact that you do not think very much of yourself, mainly because you cannot support yourself when challenged. You cave in and wimp out at the slightest whiff of provocation. You train people that they can disrespect you because you disrespect yourself. You find yourself in situation after situation where you say nothing and do nothing. You see your confidence dying on a daily basis. These housemates have told you, and you believe them, that the only way to survive is to play deaf, dumb and blind.

When you say something, they make you feel awkward. They leave you fumbling for words. They remind you of times when you tried to assert yourself and what happened. All the times you tried to speak up flash before your eyes. At home. At work. In the shop. Like in a horror movie, you start to sweat and shake, panic and run. They feed you lies and tell you that you are inferior to others. By doing this they drain you of any confidence you have.

"The definition of insanity is doing the same thing over and over again and expecting different results."

~Chapter Eleven~

A Normal Day In The Big Brother House

So, there you have it. These are your twelve unruly chattering housemates. They never stop talking in your head, vying for your attention. They all want to be you. They all want to speak on your behalf. You can't make a decision because everything has to go through each housemate before you can decide anything. The lower ranking housemates are passed over pretty quickly then it goes to the middle ranking guys for further input. By the time it gets to the higher ranking housemates you are thoroughly exhausted. Ideas come and go because they are met with objections. Dreams are thwarted because they are greeted with ridicule. Any notion you may have of leading your own life is met with emotional outbursts and running around in your head until they run out of steam.

Any issue, no matter how big or small, gets the Big Brother house treatment. Let's say it is something really simple.

Scenario: It's raining

Free Child: "Oh wow, it's raining."

Critical Parent: "You'll never find the umbrella; I told you... you should always put your umbrella in one place so that you can find it!"

Little Professor: "I wonder if I could phone in sick... I think I could get away with it. I haven't phoned in sick for ages."

Nurturing Parent: "Don't worry if you get caught in the rain, a little bit of rain won't harm you."

Free Child: "It's fun! I actually like the feel of the rain."

Critical Parent: "Oh shut up and go and look for the umbrella."

Archetypes: "I bet Jane doesn't have this problem in the morning searching for an umbrella."

Adapted Child: "I don't know what to do."

Cognitive Dissonance: "It's only a little bit of rain, it shouldn't do me any harm…But what if I catch flu?"

Little Professor: "Then you could have three weeks off work"

Ego: "The rain will mess up your new coat… why does it have to rain today of all days?"

Identity: "I don't know whether to go look for an umbrella or take a chance."

Beliefs: "It is important you arrive at work on time."

Emotions: "I hate the fricking rain!"

What do you think are the chances of you being on time for work with that debate going on inside your head?

Or

You want to ask someone out on a date.

Critical Parent: "Don't do it. You will make a fool of yourself."

Archetype: "She is just right for me. She looks like a supermodel!"

Ego: "Everyone will be impressed that she is my girlfriend. Perfect body… perfect hair…what more could a guy want?"

Free Child: "Wow, she's gorgeous and she's smiling at me... I think!"

Critical Parent: "She's not smiling at you, fool."

Belief: "If you like someone, what is wrong with letting them know?"

Ego: "She will have information on you that she could use against you in the future."

Emotions: "This is scary."

Cognitive Dissonance: "I'm going to ask her out…No I'm not... I 'm going to ask her out... No I'm not."

Little Professor: "I think the thing to do is to make her laugh…"

Adapted Child: "If I talk to her I will get tongue-tied."

Nurturing Parent: "Why don't you ask her, what have you got to lose?"

Critical Parent: "Your pride, that's what."

Identity: "I don't know what to do... she's out of my league."

What are the chances of you asking that person out for a date, do you think?

Or

You are asked to say something about the project you have been working on at the team meeting.

Critical Parent: "See I knew this would happen. Instead of going out for drinks last night you should have prepared for this. You are useless!"

Nurturing Parent: "Just do your best. Just stick to what you know about the project."

Archetypes: "This presentation needs to be word-perfect."

Cognitive Dissonance: "I think I could do a good job here...but what if you mess it up...then what?"

Free Child: "Help!"

Adapted Child: "Oh crikey, all those people looking at me..."

Ego: "Why didn't my boss tell me about this before, maybe he's trying to set me up?"

Little Professor: "If I do a good job and make it a little complicated perhaps I could ask for promotion."

Emotion: "My hands are shaking; my heart is pumping out of my chest. I think I' m going to be sick."

Beliefs: "It is always important to be ready for such occasions. 'Be prepared' is the motto my father used to say."

Identity: "I don't know what to do and I don't know where to start. Giving presentations just isn't me."

Critical Parent: "You are such a fool."

What do you think are the chances of your presentation going well with all that raucous going on inside your head?

Do you see how difficult it is for you to do anything in the collective reality? Whatever you do you have to defer to the twelve housemates and their chums who reside in your head and who demand your constant attention. By the time you listen to all their concerns, the moment is gone. They come up with so many reasons why you shouldn't do something you lose motivation. Does it feel as if you are going crazy sometimes? The housemates will not give you any peace at all. What these guys do with all their noise and raucousness is to starve you of your experience of life. They are your energy stealers. If you have a goal, they talk you out of it because they don't like change. If you want to do anything different they bring up all the things that could go wrong so that you become paralysed with fear. They feed you on a daily basis a diet of fear and in doing so these housemates have you just were they want you.

It would be logical I guess, on some level to kick all of the housemates out. That wouldn't work. You need those guys actually. They make up your personality. That is the part of you that interfaces with the collective reality. To lose any one of them would be like cutting off a leg or an arm. You just wouldn't do it.

As I said to you before, to understand anything you have to look at it. You have to be the observer. You have to know what it does, when it does it and under what circumstances it does it. You have to become aware of every dimension of your personality so that all is in accord, not fighting against each other for position or favour.

The answer here is not to throw them out or banish them from your mind for ever. The answer is to take your rightful position as owner and head of your mind. You have to learn to control your mind so that it does what you want it to do and not the other way around.

Here's how…

~Part Two~

"We can't solve problems by using the same kind of thinking we used when we created them."

~Chapter Twelve~

Putting Your House In Order...Let's Go!

You may have noticed that I am talking to you. Your housemates are of no real consequence to me. Neither should they be of any to you. You are the one that needs to get your own house in order so you can fulfil your part of the bargain.

Your part of the bargain is to live your life to your full potential. In the grand scheme of things, you were not born to have a mediocre near-life experience.

Where have you been? What have you been doing?

Do you realise that every single element that exists is represented in your body? You are earth, wind, fire and water. You are at the top of Mother Nature's tree. You have been given a brain second to none. No one can think or approach a problem like you do. You are the sum total of your experiences. You are unique. There is no one on this planet remotely like you. You are the one that beats your heart. You come from the best. Pure energy!

How does nature know when to make it night, make the flowers grow or change the seasons? Is it all organised chaos? I don't think so. Everything that happens in nature follows universal laws. You are also subject to these laws. Your body is subject to laws. Your body needs to flow in a certain way. The veins take blood towards the heart and the arteries take blood away from the heart. There is no way you can change that law.

Now just as there are laws for just about everything, there are also laws for the mind. They are called mental laws and there are four of them.

The first mental law is: *Whatever you believe with feeling becomes your experience in the collective reality*. If you believe that people are not to be trusted, you will come across people who demonstrate to you on a daily basis how untrustworthy they are. That's what you are looking out for. That is what you see and that is finally what you get. Your housemates feel good that they have kept you secure and safe.

The second mental law is: *You are like a living magnet. You attract the events and people that come into your life.* But wait! Before you get too excited about this...it is a universal law, which means that whatever you think and feel, so shall you attract. People have run away with this law, only taking the bit that they like and of course the easy bit. They think that if they construct a list of all the things they want then it will just happen. Magic! People then get so frustrated when it doesn't work. They conclude that it's all hocus-pocus. I am here to tell you that it does work. But in order for it to work you have to make sure your mind is as beautiful as the beauty that you want to attract into your life. You'd better make sure that your mind is as free flowing as the abundance that you want to flow into your life. You need to be as sharp and smart as the whizz kid you want to attract into your life. I could go on and on. And here comes the biggy... you need to love yourself as much as you want that person to love you.

Amazing people not only want to hang out with amazing people, they want to hang out with people that know that they are amazing. Dealing with folk who don't know who they are is far too energy-consuming for amazing people.

The third mental law is the law of correspondence. This law is closely associated with the laws of attraction. This law states that *whatever is going on in your virtual world will be reflected in your collective reality.* Lack of confidence in the collective reality means low self-esteem in your virtual world. Stress in the collective reality means imbalance in your virtual world. Remember the old adage: tidy desk, tidy mind? It is exactly that!

And this is exactly the point; if you are not getting the

most out of your life then you have to look inside. In fact, you have to go inside and give your mind an upgrade so that your mind energy matches the energy you want to attract in the physical world.

The fourth mental law is *that you will become whatever you think about over time.* Let me explain:

Once I was coming home from a business trip tired and worn out. I don't normally go on the walking conveyor belt at the airport but I was tired. It is customary that the people who want to stand keep to the right and those who want to continue walking go to the left. Well, I was one of those who wanted to keep walking to get out of the airport as soon as I could, but there was this elderly man in front of me, blocking my way. "Excuse me," I said very politely, "Could I get past you?"

Anyone would think that I had asked him to drop his trousers.

"No you can't," he said almost spitting at me. "What do you think I am doing here...waiting for a bus?"

His energy was so toxic that it hung in the air. It showed on his face, in his demeanour and in the way he walked. He was like an angry lizard waiting to strike at the world. He frightened everyone in his path. He frightened me! This was a guy coming *back* from holiday; would you want to meet him before he went? What had the collective reality done to him to make him so aggressive? He was miserable and he looked miserable and all that he saw was misery. There is no way he could have been thinking thoughts of good tidings of comfort and joy and at the same time give me a mouthful of hate. It's very funny but when people say that they are going to give so and so a piece of their minds that is exactly what they are doing. You see a piece of people's minds every day. What does your mind say about you? If you think horrible things you will become a horrible person.

The first thing that you have to do is take charge of your mind. Your mind is not a physical thing. You can't see it, or touch it, yet you know it is there. It is virtual, a concept, a metaphor or a hypothesis. You cannot apply the laws of logic to it. They do not apply. When you apply thinking to thinking you get more thinking. You overthink. You think things through. You obsess. Being intelligent is not only about how smart you are; it is also about how you use your smartness. There is a difference.

I meet superbright people like you every day. Some really smart cookies, I can tell you. They have degrees, family, friends, and good jobs and still they tell me they are not happy with themselves or their achievements. Still they get the feeling that they are flying their ship at half-mast…

How can it be that such smart people do not use their smartness to design the life that they want? I don't get it. How come there are people who can give facts and figures on the most obscure topics yet they are unable to talk about their feelings? How is it that they know stuff about stuff that will never impact their world and yet they don't know how they think, what they think and why they think the way they do? I call that weird science!

Imagine you were watching a movie. The main character, Mr Beano, goes to the doctor and the doctor tells him he's got thrombosis. What would Mr Beano think if the doctor said any of the following?

"You have thrombosis but it doesn't matter."

Or

"You have thrombosis but just forget it."

Or

"You have thrombosis, but put it to the back of your mind."

Or

"Let's see if you can find someone to blame."

Or

"You have thrombosis and you are a bad person."

You see how ridiculous all of these responses sound. If someone told you that you had something wrong with your body, you would never take it lying down. You would probably want a diagnosis and a prognosis. So how come you have accepted the neurosis of your mind without challenge?

You have the potential to go inside your mind and give it a spring clean. You can free yourself of the neuroses that lurk within. Low self-esteem, lack of confidence, stress and fears of just about everything are neuroses of the mind and are not natural. Yet you have come to believe that they are. They are not. The true nature of your mind is clear, bright, fast, fresh and creative. Your mind has the same potential as Einstein, Gandhi, Bill Gates, Michaelangelo; the only difference between you and them is that they used their minds as they were intended.

Don't you think it is time for you to show up? You have been there lying low amongst all the housemates all the time. Being pushed around and overruled.

It is time to move from the back of the house to the head of the house where you rightfully belong. It is time for you to find your voice. I know I have said it before and I want to say it again. Getting rid of the housemates is not the answer. You need those guys. What would you do if you didn't have Fear or Anger? You need them to help you if you are ever in a tight spot. You do not, however, need them on a daily basis. Unless of course you live on the Serengeti and you have to cross paths with all sorts of wildlife. Your job is to keep those somewhat unruly housemates in check.

You are going to rule the roost. You are going to invite some of *your* chums to move in with you and sit at the rightful place at the head of the table. You are not declaring war on the housemates but you have to tell them in no uncertain terms what you want their roles and responsibilities to be.

There is good news and bad news. The bad news first: when you decide to take up your rightful place at the helm of the house, that action is going to put all the housemates' noses out of joint. They are not going to like it one bit. Be prepared for all sorts of rants and raving in your head. There will be an explosion of fears and doubts. The housemates hate change and they will try every trick in the book to have you stay as you were. They don't want their hold on you dislodged. When you finally show up, they will not like it one bit. None of them will want to lose status. Anger will become angry. Fear will be fearful. Blame will blame. All of them will be in uproar. Mind your head, hold your nerve and keep going.

You know that day follows night, so after a storm there must be a calm.

For the next 21 days when you follow the Mind Synergy program, things will feel strange. You will step outside your comfort zone. The comfort zone is called that for a reason. Everything is safe and predictable inside. The housemates know exactly what to say and how to react to any given situation in the collective reality. Now you are going to teach them new skills. Skills that reflect who you are. Be prepared to feel self-conscious as you try things out.

The term 'self-consciousness' means consciousness or awareness of oneself. That is a good thing. Being self-conscious is your feedback to yourself that you are stretching and growing.

The only way for a butterfly to be is for the caterpillar to break free from the larvae that confines it. Housemate Emotions will be very emotional. Critical Parent will throw every rule book at you. Adapted Child will be very afraid that you might upset others. The Ego will be hopping up and down as he sees his power diminish. All of them will have something to say. All of them want you to go hide in the corner again.

Let me say this, if you back down now and agree to their definition of you, it will be ten times harder should you choose to make a stand in the future. Why? Because each of them will know you do not have any follow through and if pushed you'll back down.

So don't back down!

The good news is that every day that passes you will feel different. You will feel freer and a little lighter. Your mind will become clearer. You will be able to think and create at a deeper level. Your virtual reality will start to become balanced with the collective reality… and so there will be no stress and strain, just a flow of your energy.

So here we go….

Oh and just before you go into the old chestnut, "Oh nothing is going to happen", then all I ask of you is to give it a try. Did you know that there is a dune in the Arcachon Bay area in France, which happens to be the tallest dune in the Europe? The most fascinating thing about the dune is that it is actually walking across the territory. It is continuous in its movements; sometimes it moves faster and sometimes slowly, but it is moving nonetheless. It has covered over 20 houses, roads and trees.

Furthermore, did you also know that there are mountain goats that live in the Argon region of Morocco? At first as you approach the trees you would be forgiven for thinking that they are the tree's blossoms – albeit rather large blossoms – but if you venture closer you will see that they are goats, standing upright in the trees. As casual as you please, and hanging on by their hoof tips. I tell you this for you to understand that the impossible is nothing and nothing is impossible. It's an old cliché but you know what I mean.

Now it is time for you to put your house in order. You have to bring out the skills that I know you already have to live your life how you want to. There is nothing I can give you, show you or teach you. You have it all inside you. You cannot get lemonade from an orange or blood from a stone. With the same token, I cannot tell you anything about yourself that you do not on some level already know. What I do is remind you.

Over the next 21 days I invite you to follow the 21-day

Mind Synergy program. What have you got to lose?

The exercises, unless otherwise stated, are to be done to yourself, with yourself and by yourself, in your head. This is an inside job. No one else is going to fix you. You could read a thousand books or attend a trillion courses; they will only work in part. You have to go inside. There is no other way to undo the years of indoctrination. Don't worry; you are not going to brainwash yourself. Well, not in a bad way. In the next 21 days you are going to take the opportunity to clean up your act. You will go over all the rules, regulations and messages that you have ever received, absorbed and digested. Overtly or covertly, directed or indirectly. Some of them you will welcome and keep and some of them you will banish. You may find values, virtues and beliefs that have lain dormant or you didn't know you had. The ones you keep are the ones that truly define you as you wish to be defined. They will all flow in your direction. That is to say, every fibre of your being will flow to support each other and in doing so they will support you. It is then that you will experience the synergistic nature of your mind. You will free the ties that bind you to mediocrity. You will be lighter. The exercises are designed to allow all of this to happen!

By the end of these exercises, activities and drills you will be able:

- ✓ To challenge situations and events in your life assertively, rather than cower and withdraw.
- ✓ To develop the courage to persevere with your goals, rather than give up.
- ✓ To act with integrity and dignity, rather than expedience.
- ✓ To take responsibility for your actions in whatever you do rather than shake it off.
- ✓ To embrace your reality rather than retreat from it.
- ✓ To move forward in your life rather than live in the past or in the future.

✓ To use your creativity to the full.
✓ To be positive and loving.
✓ To deal with your demons rather than let your demons deal with you.
✓ To treat yourself with the utmost respect at all times.
✓ To be free of stress.

You are about to welcome four new housemates and their chums to your virtual world. They are your new friends. You and they are going to get very close. They are called: Courage, Values, Your energy, Your self-esteem, Your emotional intelligence. You also have some lovely assistants to help you. They are called: No mind, No opinion, Listening, Saying No, Goals and passion and lastly, Confidence. Together with these guys you are going to develop an amazing sense of yourself which is strong, decisive and positive and which serves as a great springboard from which you can release your creativity and potential.

"Great spirits have always found violent opposition from mediocrities. The latter cannot understand it when a man does not thoughtlessly submit to hereditary prejudices but honestly and courageously uses his intelligence."

~Chapter Thirteen~

New Housemate: Your Courage

My nephew Mickey is a stand-up comedian. I asked him how he could stand in front of a group of strangers and profess to make them laugh. This would be my worst nightmare! He told me that as he waits to go on, he has to 'psyche' himself up to find the 'sweet spot'. He's waiting for his name to be called to go on stage. He feels the adrenalin sweep over his body. Sweat! Everything in his body tells him to run. Yet he is prepared and he has waited and dreamt of this moment all his life. He stands firm in the moment. He waits for the 'sweet spot.'

The sweet spot is feeling the fear and letting it surge through you, like currents of electricity, around you and finally over you. You know it cannot and will not kill you. The sweet spot is at *that* moment when particle meets wave, and when wave meets particle. It is at that moment when the components of energy combine to create more than the sum of their parts. Synergy. At this moment you step into your potential and magic happens. Everything slows down. You observe what is happening from a distance and yet at the same time you are in the moment. You are the moment. You and time are one. You and whatever you are doing has merged. It is then that you know yourself as what you are. Energy. The sweet spot is where your emotions and your desires meet.

You say:

I don't know what got into me."

"I saw sparks…"

"I set the house on fire."

"I was floating on air."

"It was like a dream."
"It was as if time stood still."
"I was in the zone."
"It blew my mind."
"It was magical."
"I was moved…"

It is important to distinguish where the sweet spot is. Energy has no time. So it cannot be measured. Can you put a time on creativity? Creativity comes when it is ready. Neither can you put a time on passion. The sweet spot comes *where* you place your awareness, your attention and your focus. If you want to enjoy the sweet spot, you have to go where the action is. Where is where? Where is at the crossroads of preparation and faith. You just do your thing. Gather your knowledge, skills and experience and wait. Your have faith because you know that opportunities will show up sooner or later. You have to wait for the wave to come, hop on and ride.

What is the thing that my nephew has in spades? That causes him to get up on stage before strangers, in strange locations all hours of the day and night and dare to make them laugh? It is courage. The courage to step over the line of your comfort zone, feel the force of emotions, clap your hands together like a boxer and say, "Let's do this…"

Courage is when you observe the situation and make a choice of how to react. Courage is a decision to slip into the 'sweet spot' which lies between fear and anger and feel the full force of the transformation of these emotions into potential energy!

Courage is the absence of giving up or giving in. Courage is called upon whenever you confront a difficult, frightening, painful or disturbing situation. When your resources are challenged or pushed to the absolute limit.

Courage is not about being brave. That is a different issue. For example, it is brave to save someone from drowning or a burning house. It is also brave to have to suffer a lot of pain through illness or injury. Hopefully, they do not happen too often in the grand scheme of things.

You need courage every single day of life. The word *courage* comes from the French root *cour* or *coeur*, which means heart. So courage has to do with the heart, that vital muscle that keeps your blood flowing and sustains life. Without courage you have a near-life experience. How would you know your heart was there if it wasn't beating in your chest? But what is the purpose of your heart? Just to keep you alive, in other words to beat 2.5 billion times until it can't do it anymore and stops beating? Or is its purpose for you to experience life? You go for promotion, it beats faster. The love of your life walks into the room, it flutters. You give a great presentation, it soars. You follow your dreams, it sings. How else will you know your heart, if you do not listen and follow it?

Courage is not the absence of fear, but using it, pushing through it and moving ahead of it. It is a willingness to feel the chemical rush of adrenalin and work through it, because you know that it will pass. All things must pass; it is the law of nature.

Courage is what you are left with when you mix your positive energy with your willingness to succeed. Courage transmutes and controls Fear and all his chums.

You have courage; don't think for a minute that you do not. Crossing the road every day or driving in traffic requires a great deal of calculation and risk. Don't take for granted the courage that you have because it is like a muscle – the more you use it the stronger it becomes.

The Courage Gym

Exercise One: Counting your courage so far

- ✓ List three things that you have done in your life of which you are proud.
- ✓ List ten skills and abilities that you used to succeed.

It is impossible for you to quantify the rules and regulations you have taken on board since you were born. You have rules and regulations for everything. Covert and overt rules! Live and dormant rules! Rules that are difficult for you to adhere to today are difficult because they were originally designed with your grandparents in mind. In other words, they are archaic. You have rules that you don't even know you have. These rules keep you in line and teach you how to be a pillar of the establishment. You are in a double bind. Abiding by the rules leaves you frustrated and limited and breaking the rules leaves you feeling guilty. Figuring out which rules work for you and which ones don't is an endless task. Some of these rules work for you and that's good and you should keep them. I am not saying break the rules, that would be ridiculous. Some of the rules pertaining to your culture and family are important to keep. Neither do you have time to go over every rule to see if it works for you or not.

Here is an exercise which allows you to balance the rules and regulations of being in your collective reality and being true to who you are.

Here are your new beliefs. These beliefs override any ideas that you hold about yourself, consciously or subconsciously, that do not serve you and the way you want to live. These new beliefs support you in every way.

Exercise Two: Changing rules to beliefs

You need to get really familiar with these new beliefs of yours. There are four of them. Repeat them over and over to yourself until you know them by heart. Chant them while you are walking or waiting in a queue. Recite them to yourself before you drop off to sleep. In fact, that is an excellent time to do it. Set the words to your favourite tune. Repeat them back to front. Chant them as a monk in a monastery chants his prayers. Repeat 21 times a day for 21 days…and wait!

Here are your new beliefs.

- ✓ I believe in me…
- ✓ I believe that all things are possible…
- ✓ I believe in the power of my virtual reality and my power potential in the collective reality…
- ✓ I believe in the sanctity of nature and all creatures great and small.

After you start to see a difference in your energy levels, you may wish to do the advanced version of this exercise.

I believe in me…because (start with one and every day find a new reason why you believe in you), e.g. I believe in me…because I am a good person. Add as many comments about yourself as you can think of.

Exercise Three: Developing more courage

Listed below are 32 courage builders. Each builder has a score rating. Your challenge is to do any one of these builders and get to 100 as fast as you can without injury! Good luck!

	Courage builder	Rating
1.	Take a course.	2
2.	Bake a cake and take it to work.	2
3.	Learn 200 words of a new language.	2
4.	Test-drive a luxury car.	5
5.	End a relationship that drains you or hurts you.	5
6.	Take a painting or photography class.	5

7.	Learn how to give amazing presentations.	10
8.	Get fit and healthy.	15
9.	Invite your friends over for a dinner party.	5
10.	Give at least five people a compliment today.	5
11.	Learn the words to your favourite song and sing it to a friend.	10
12.	Hire a life coach or a personal trainer.	10
13.	Write an article and seek to get it published.	15
14.	Give eye contact to everyone you speak to for a day.	5
15.	Smile 21 times in the day (count them).	5
16.	Turn your hobby into a 'pop-up' business for 21 days.	15
17.	Volunteer your services at work, university or school, to teach a workshop on something you know how to do.	15
18.	Visit another city in your country for the weekend.	10
19.	Make a business card and letterhead.	5
20.	Eat at an ethnic restaurant that you have never tried before.	5
21.	Say your prayers. Have a conversation with God.	10
22.	Take different routes to work each day for 21 days. See how many you can find.	5
23.	Go to a nursing home and visit people who need company.	10
24.	Quit smoking.	20
25.	Take a dance class.	10

26.	Go to the theatre alone.	5
27.	Tell your favourite joke in public.	10
28.	Pick one incomplete task in your life (cluttered attic, article you want to write, craft you want to begin) and do it for 15 minutes a day. It's more courageous to do something for a small chunk of time and do it again the very next day. than it is to sit back and say it can't be done because you don't have enough time.	10
29.	Ask for a promotion.	20
30.	Participate in an open-mic night or sing karaoke.	20
31.	Tell someone you love them.	20
32.	Book an amazing holiday.	25

What is your final score?

☐

Exercise Four: Random acts of Courage for every day of the week

Monday
1. Say hello to five strangers as you pass them on the street.
2. Make eye contact with a stranger and don't look away until they do first.
3. Convince a stranger to have their photo taken with you.
4. Ask someone working at a supermarket for help finding an item.
5. Learn a song and sing it to a friend.

Tuesday
1. Wave and smile at someone you don't know (as if you do).
2. Go the wrong way up or down an escalator.

3. Go to a bar on your own and strike up a conversation with someone as they do in the movies.
4. Ask someone you like for their mobile number.
5. Strike up a conversation with a homeless person on the street.

Wednesday
1. Unfriend someone annoying on Facebook, or send a friend request to someone you've only met briefly but wish to know better.
2. Walk into a tall building and ask at reception if you can go up on the roof to look at the view.
3. Haggle over the price of something.
4. Speak up and make a suggestion at a work meeting.
5. Correct anyone who mispronounces your name.

Thursday
1. Strike up a conversation with a stranger and find out 1) their greatest fear and 2) their greatest passion.
2. Hold a conversation with a stranger for three minutes or more.
3. Get back in contact with a childhood friend/mentor and thank them for the positive impact they've had on your life.
4. Give five people a compliment today.
5. Say hello every time you walk into an occupied elevator.

Friday
1. Donate ten items that you do not use to charity.
2. Visit a park or museum that you've never been to before.
3. Eat something you've never eaten before, or try a new recipe.

4. Get on a random bus. Get off after five stops. Find your way home.
5. Take a class in something you've never tried before.

Use the weekend to reflect on which activity was easy for you, which one made your heart skip and beat and which ones were actually fun!

If you want to work your courage out some more, then on Monday just start again, or better still, invent your own.

Exercise Five: Know yourself

It is important to know yourself. You need to have a PHD on you.

Have a go at answering these questions. Get yourself a nice drink of something and settle back and answer the questions as you want to answer and not as you think you should answer. Be honest with yourself. Have fun!

1. What is your purpose in life?
2. If you could change one thing about yourself what would you change and why?
3. If you could do any job in the world what would it be and why?
4. If you could live anywhere in the world where would you live and why?
5. What are you looking for in life... a) love b) power c) adventure d) respect e) money f) excitement or g) something else?
6. If you could wake up tomorrow having gained a superpower, what would it be?
7. Would you trade places with anyone on this planet? Who and why?
8. Do you believe in a greater force? Explain.
9. What is the purpose of a relationship?

10. What do you bring to your relationships?
11. Why do relationships sometimes go wrong in your opinion?
12. How do you take care of your mind, body and spirit?
13. What makes you angry?
14. What makes you sad?
15. What is the scariest thing you have ever had to do? What did you learn about yourself?
16. How happy are you now? (Scale of 1 -10). What needs to be in place to take you to the next level? Make a list.
17. What is your ideal life?
18. What makes you laugh?
19. What is the one thing in life that you regret?
20. What gives you joy?

"There comes a time when the mind takes a higher plane of knowledge but can never prove how it got there."

~Chapter Fourteen~

New Housemate: Your Values

Values are about what is important to you in your life. Values are the reasons why you do the things you do. The values in your virtual world have to be compatible with the values you exhibit and experience from others in the collective reality. If there is no compatibility, you will not be happy.

If you value freedom and expression and your partner is jealous and possessive, that relationship will be a struggle. If you value your family and friends but your boss wants you to work weekends and all hours, chances are you will be looking for a new job. If you value integrity but your friend never does what she says she is going to do, chances are the relationship will be strained.

You probably aren't aware of your values, most people aren't either. You are only aware of the bad feeling you get after a situation. That bad feeling or bitter taste in your mouth is what you get when you betray yourself.

It is paramount to know your values. How can you defend that which is important to you if you do not know what is important to you? If you do not know what is important to you, you leave yourself open for people to violate your values all the time. It's not their fault. How are they to know if you do not tell them? Smiling sweetly through the abuse and bullying doesn't work anymore, it is time to stand up and be counted for what you believe in.

Exercise Six: Know your values

Here are 23 objects that you may value above all else and things that are important to you. Tick the top five that you believe represent who you are.

1. Family	2. Freedom	3. Integrity	4. Money	5. Faith	6. Relation-ship	7. Truth
8. Health	9. Spiritua-lity	10. Advent-ure	11. Trust	12. Ambition	13. Religion	14. Pleasure
15. Power	16. Knowl-edge	17. Fame	18. Respect	19. Loyalty	20. Kindness	21. Friends
22. Fun	23. Love	24. Add your own	25. Add your own			

List your top five values here.
   1.
   2.
   3.
   4.
   5.

With your top five values in mind, imagine that your plane has crashed in the Amazonian jungle. There are no survivors, just you. You sit on a rock, contemplating your fate. You have no food or water and you fear you will die. Just as these morbid thoughts start to take over your mind, you see a pair of huge eyes staring at you from behind a bush. You are excited that there is life deep in the Amazon and where there is life, there is hope. Right? You tell the little boy in front of you that you need to get back to your country and he stretches out his hand. You realise he wants paying. You have no collateral with which to bargain. The only thing you can give him is one of your five values.
   Which one do you give up? _____

The little boy disappears into the jungle along with your value. He soon reappears with who you can only describe as an 'Elder'. He tells you that if you hurry you can get to the water's edge, where you can pick up a boat that will take you to a smallholding where you can catch your plane. You get up but before you set off he too asks for a value.

Which one do you give him? _____

The 'Elder' takes you to the water's edge and tell you to wait. As you stare into the water you imagine all sorts of dangerous animals in there. Alligators! Piranha! So swimming is not an option then! Suddenly you notice the water starting to ripple and you know the boat man is coming. He beckons you on board and at the same time stretches his bony hand out for a value. This is his payment.

Which one do you give him? _____

He takes you to the smallholding where you can get a plane to take you back to your country and your collective reality. You do not have any money and plane tickets cost money. The only things you have left are your two values. Which one will you use for the plane fare and which one will you take home with you?

Which one do you give up? _____
Which one stays with you? _____

What you have completed is an exercise in prioritising your values. It is not as easy as it may seem, I know, but now you know the reason why you do the things you do! You have values and so does everyone in the collective reality. It is important for you to honour your values. These are the rules you stand by, not just the ones handed down to you. Honouring your values means you honour yourself.

Exercise Seven: Skills analysis

List 20 skills that you have.
I'll give you a few examples.
Driving
Cooking
Coaching
Speaking another language
Dancing
Playing a musical instrument
Now answer these questions:
Choose a skill from your list.
How do you do what you do?
How do you know to do what you do and when?
Break it down as much as possible.

Another example: I love to cook. I wouldn't say that I am an excellent cook, but I do love it!

I begin to cook in my mind first of all. Even before I get up in the morning, I ask myself what I would like to eat. Is there anything that we haven't had for a long time? I think about what I already have in the freezer. I ask my husband what he would like to eat as well. I check myself to see if I am up for going to the shops on a food spree. When it is time for me to cook and if I am going to cook, it's usually around 5 pm each day, the kitchen must be clean. If I am going to use a certain knife, that knife needs to be in its rightful position. Everything must be in the start position. I start at the end. So if I am going to make a dessert I will do that first. I never get everything I need out of the cupboards, as to me that would be a *fait accompli*. What I want to do with my cooking is create. So I never know what the final flavour will be. The creation is spontaneous. Sometimes I pretend that I am a guest on a cooking program, usually Jamie Oliver. You'd think me mad if you came into my home and overheard me talking to myself about the virtues of dicing onions as opposed to slicing them. I seldom, if ever, put the food on the plate. I prefer to put my creations on serving platters for people to help themselves. I always cook too much. I always have a glass of wine with the meal. My husband and I always eat together facing each other every night. It is a ritual. It is an activity. It is intimacy. It is our opportunity to regroup.

By doing this exercise you get to understand how your mind works when you do the things you love to do. You also get to see and feel your mind in action when there is no overthinking, doubt, indecisions, criticism. You get to experience flow.

You can do this exercise as many times as you like, using different skills that you have. This is great for building a skills bank. You know what they say, "You can never have too much money in the bank." At the same token you can never have too many skills in the skills bank!

Exercise Eight: Love your flag

Consider your culture and all the things that make it great and make you proud.

List seven things you love about your culture…

Exercise Nine: Your first team

Think about your family.

List four important values passed on to you from your family that you would like to uphold...

Exercise Ten: Talking to yourself

Find a picture of yourself when you were young or much younger. Take a good look at the photo. Look at your face looking out at you from the photo as you look at you. What is that face saying and what do you want to say to that face?

"Everything is energy and that's all there is to it.
Match the frequency of the reality you want and you
cannot help but get that reality. It can be no other way.
This is not philosophy. This is physics."

~Chapter Fifteen~

New Housemate: Your Energy

Everything is energy and energy can be nothing other than positive. It can be blocked, it can be contaminated, transformed, and it can be stopped, but at its core, energy is positive. That is to say, it does what it is designed to do. Electricity flows, wind blows and flowers grow. It is in your nature to be positive. Energy flows from you in the form of your passion and creativity or it flows from you in the form of aggression or passivity. It can even seep out of you, like escaping gas in the form of sarcasm, criticism, scorn, anger and general all round party pooper. You may ask, in what way is sarcasm positive? Well it is if you consider that the sarcasm is a cover up for what's really going on…it is a coping mechanism or a protection shield from people ever getting too close.

Years ago, I was working as a therapist. It was very hard work. I had a client company who was in the business of security. Their employees are the guys that come and take the money from the banks and shops. They have reinforced vans and they are heavily armoured. The bad guys always seem to find a way to get to them, though. It was my job to deal with the PTSD. That is, Post Traumatic Stress Disorder. I remember one client that came to see me who was so aggressive towards me, it was difficult to ask him questions. He was a bit like the guy on the airport conveyer belt. I used to dread Monday mornings because I knew he was coming for his session. I struggled to see why he came, as all he did was rant and rave. But I was there and the robbers were not. How else was he going to get his utter shame and disgust with himself out of his system? His energy was blocked.

One day I saw a chink in his armour and I decided to go for it. During this session he started to cry. I must say I was taken aback. He told me how he felt as if the robbers had cut off his manhood. He wasn't Bruce Willis or Arnie Schwarzenegger. He was just a regular guy who had peed himself when the robber had put a sawn-off shot gun into his mouth. He spoke of how he felt like a coward and how he couldn't face anyone because he thought that they thought that he was a pussy. He was a guy that had let the image that he had of himself down. He wasn't angry with the system. He was disappointed and ashamed of himself. I asked him if he had his time over, what would he do? And he told me he would have had a go. I spoke to him about the fact that he would be a dead hero and his children would never see his face again. I told him that he was a hero in my eyes. I told him that one day he would be able to tell his story to his grandchildren himself, and that is heroism. I never saw him again.

Energy is never negative; it is blocked, polluted or transformed into something else which you interpret as negative. All energy must flow. If a tree falls in the river, the water will mount up at this point until it finds a way to get past the tree. It must go around, over or underneath. After years of going over or around the tree, the river will forge a new path, cut into the land or create an undercurrent beneath the water. After several years, if the tree is removed do you think that the river will just go back to the former path? No, it will not and it cannot!

This happens in humans as well. If you have had an argument with someone and you tell them what you think … this is a flow of energy. The problem arises if you do not tell them what you think and you keep the information inside. Some people can store stuff for years, are you one of them? If you are, this means you can hold on to grudges and wrongs for years, waiting for the opportunity to vent. When that particular moment comes, all hell is let loose. It is as if the dam has busted. You bring up everything and anything that has happened to you to do with that topic – past, present and future. Whoosh!

Just one more example to get my point across and so that you are in no doubt what I think about energy. When you watch the Discovery channel and you observe the lions on the Serengeti about to make a kill, is this negative energy? No, it is the circle of life. The lion understands his collective reality and what he is born to do. You have to understand yours!

If you are reading these words, chances are you are amongst the 10% of the world population who do not have to get up in the morning and wonder if they will eat or not. Ten percent; think about it!

Instead of counting your blessings and looking for ways to expand, the opposite seems to be true. You look at what you don't have rather than what you do have. Your world becomes small instead of your oyster. You get on a treadmill of work and grind. Your only respite is two weeks holiday every year if you are lucky. Is that what it is all about? Is that the meaning of your life? To find a job were you can experience mediocrity on a daily basis? You are part of the privileged 10% of the world's population. Doesn't that stand for something? Should it not mean something? You have already won a gold medal right there.

Do you remember the man at the airport who nearly took my head off when I asked him to excuse me?

That poor man at the airport was demonstrating how much pain he was in. How much he had got it wrong. It was him against the world. His sword was his tongue. If anyone said anything out of sorts to him, he whiplashed them with his trusty weapon. It is hard to believe, but this man who, without a moment's thought, had gone to his default mode of hostility, had once been a child. Once he had been open, trusting and full of potential. He believed the rules and regulations instilled in him to the point where he became them. How disappointed he was with the whole show. Two weeks in Spain could never overcome a life of thwarted energy. I thought about him at Immigration. I was overcome with sadness for him. I noticed too, that he was alone, shuffling along in the queue. Not for him the small talk, banter and laughter that reminds you that you are alive. I wanted to give him a hug. I decided against it as I don't much care for hospital food.

The point I want to make is that energy that flows, moves easily and free, vibrates at a higher frequency. It is natural. It is pure and simple. It is leaner. It is faster. When you vibrate at a higher frequency you can see opportunities where others see none. You can seize the day! The opportunity seeds that you sow create other opportunities, and so on and so forth. Your life then becomes full of abundance. Imagine if you were vibrating at a higher frequency. What would you do? Start your own business? Show your photography? Exhibit your art? Learn to sing? Learn to dance? Learn to swim? Learn all three! Join a theatre group? Learn a skill? Follow your passion? Jump out of an aeroplane (parachute included)? Go see Australia? Say I'm sorry? Forgive and forget? Say I love you?

Exercise Eleven: Positive energy flow

Apply the properties of energy to yourself. Say these statements to yourself at least once a day…

"I am positive…"

"I am faster…"

"I am pure and simple…"

"I am lean and strong…"

"I am energy…"

And now:

Say the positive statements to yourself and now add the word 'because.'

For example:

"I am positive…because …I see every opportunity as a learning experience."

"I am faster...because…."

You may feel a little stupid repeating this mantra to yourself. But I want you to know that what you are releasing here is the energy required to unleash your confidence. I hope you know it's worth it. For the best ever results recite the mantra to yourself when you go for your walks, or when you are waiting in a queue.

I now want to talk about the laws of attraction. It fits neatly here. I think I may have given the impression that I wasn't a fan of the laws of attraction. I need to clarify this. I believe in the laws of attraction but not the way that it is portrayed by some. That is to say, I do not think that if you create a mood board or make a list of the perfect partner that you want in your life that it will happen. Not because of the list anyway.

You are a magnetic being. Your brain has a magnetic field. If your nerves and muscles didn't constantly generate tiny electric currents you wouldn't be here. There are certain people who can't wear a watch, and I've heard of others whose 'electricity' can interfere with delicate electrical equipment such as computers.

Some creatures, such as the electric eel, can produce excessive amounts of electromagnetism, even enough to kill. Others, such as hammerhead sharks, can sense, and home in on, the tiny electromagnetic field of their prey's gill movements as the fish tries to hide under the sand. I have had the privilege of swimming with dolphins and all I had to do was pat the water and the dolphin would appear. So you see the laws of attraction are a little bit more complicated than just writing a list. You are a living magnet, but unless you have your house in tiptop order, you are only going to attract a mirror image of yourself.

People make all sorts of lists about what they want in their lives, thinking that just by saying it or focusing on it, it will magically appear.

They say:

"I have no money. I need more money."

"I want the perfect lover."

"I want a better job."

Let's just take a look at these three wants:

I want more money

I heard a famous singer once talk about his life. He stated that when he was poor and down-and-out he had to struggle for everything. He slept on people's sofas and had to scrounge every meal. Now that he is rich and famous, he never has to ask for a thing. People give him cars to drive, his meals are invariably free at fancy restaurants and girls throw themselves at him. The point is this: money is an entity that has its own force field. Money is attracted to money. When you say to yourself and the collective reality that you have no money, what you are expressing is lack. What you will attract is more lack or the feeling of lack.

I want the perfect partner

First of all, perfection doesn't exist. Things are perfect because they are not perfect. That is what makes life interesting. I would imagine that the perfect anything would be extremely boring. If everything was perfect then how would you get motivated? There would be no reason to try.

Anyway, if you want the perfect partner you would need to be perfect yourself in every way. Like attracts like. The only way to attract anyone anywhere near the standards you are looking for is to raise your own game. Only when you work on yourself will you attract people into your life that correspond with your thoughts and beliefs. Whilst working on yourself, you may come to realise that the things you thought were important in a partner may not be quite as important as you once imagined.

I want a better job

What about if you want a better job? Better than what? If you ask for something and you expect the collective reality to respond you need to be as specific as possible. It is also important not to focus on the wrong thing.

I have a huge multinational corporation as a client. This company's business model is to recruit people on a contractual basis at first, mainly to check them out. Usually I train these 'newbies' as they are called, within the first year of service. Naturally, they want to know as much about the company as possible. For some reason, I would say 95% become fixated on becoming a full time employee. They become competitive and secretive. They become very sycophantic. It's not comfortable to watch. When it comes to asking me what they need to do to become a full time employee, I always reply in the same way. Do your job. If you do your job to the best of your ability, you will become a full time employee. The company didn't employ you to see how competitive or conniving you can be. They employed you to do your job. If you do that you will be rewarded.

It could be that you are in the wrong job. It could be that the people you work with do not recognise your talent. Just let your energy flow, like a river, and you will see. Just do your thing and you will see! All the time spent doing your job will never be wasted. My mother wanted me to be a barrister. She thought I had the 'gift of the gab.' I wanted to be a singer and dancer. I dabbled with both. Now I am a trainer and none of my former studies are lost on me. I design my courses like a lawyer and I deliver them as if I was at the London O2.

If they leave you to answer the phone for most of the day, become the best phone answerer in the business. If they overwork you, spend your time thinking about how you will do it differently when you are a manager. Whatever they make you do, use the time to work on yourself. Work by day and dream by night. All of these well-known people started somewhere.

George Clooney	Door to door salesman
Simon Cowell	Post boy
Mick Jagger	Hospital porter
Danny DeVito	Hairdresser
Ozzy Osborne	Worked in a slaughter house
Demi Moore	Debt collector
Jim Carey	Cleaner
Jennifer Aniston	Telesales
Whoopi Goldberg	Morgue beautician
Kanye West	Shop assistant at Gap

George Clooney, as he went from door to door selling his wares, was always George Clooney. The world just didn't know he was George Clooney. He had to figure out a way for the world to know who he was. Same goes for you! Oh, and before you say it, you cannot be George Clooney, that role is taken!

Question: What is the difference between George Clooney, the door to door salesman, and George Clooney, the international actor and heart throb? Answer: Energy!

Allowing your energy to flow is not about being namby-pamby. Quite the opposite is true. Flow is saying to you, "I will do whatever I need to do until I achieve my goals. I am determined, disciplined and strong." If you need to study, you study. If you need to get fit and healthy, you get fit and healthy. If you need to move on because something is not working out, you move on.

I am reminded of the actor Matthew McConaughey, who had to lose 60 lbs for his role as a gay guy in the film *Dallas Buyers Club*, for which he won an Oscar. When he was asked about losing the 60 lbs he replied, "I just did what I had to do."

You may think that your brain cells and senses are located in the brain and only in the brain. That is not the case. You have little brain outposts all the way along your spinal cord. Each of these outposts looks after a particular section of your body. You talk with your mouth. Yet your stomach talks to you. Your heart speaks. My stomach speaks to me, usually in an important meeting when I have skipped lunch. Every fibre of your body has the intelligence to understand what it is doing, when it is doing it and how its actions feed into the whole. If my stomach rumbles and I eat, it is my brain *and* my stomach that feel satisfied, not just my brain.

Let's focus for a while on the energy stations. They are sometimes referred to as chakras in other disciplines. There are seven in total.

1st energy station

This energy station sits at the base of your spine, at your tailbone.

If you have physical imbalances in the 1st energy station, these may manifest as problems in the legs, feet, rectum, tailbone, immune system, male reproductive parts and prostate gland. You are also likely to experience issues of degenerative arthritis, knee pain, sciatica, eating disorders, and constipation.

If you have emotional imbalances you may worry about your ability to survive. You worry about money, food and life's necessities.

When this energy station is in balance, you feel supported, a sense of safety, a connection to the physical world, and grounded.

2nd energy station

This energy station is located two inches below your navel.

If you suffer with physical imbalances at this energy station, these may manifest as sexual and reproductive issues, urinary problems, kidney dysfunction, hip, pelvic and lower back pain.

Emotional imbalances may mean that you have problems with your relationships, your ability to express your emotions and your ability to have fun.

When this energy station is balanced, you have an ability to take risks and you are creative. You are committed. You are passionate, sexual and outgoing.

3rd energy station

This energy station is located three inches above your navel.

Physical imbalances in this energy station may result in digestive problems, liver dysfunction, chronic fatigue, high blood pressure, diabetes, stomach ulcers, pancreas and gallbladder issues and colon diseases.

Emotional imbalances here include issues of personal power and self-esteem. You are your own worst enemy and you criticise everything about yourself, from your appearance to your job, from your relationships or lack of them to where you live. Nothing is off bounds. The big issue here is the fear of rejection.

When this energy station is balanced, you feel self-respect and self-compassion. You feel in control, assertive and confident.

4th energy station

This energy station is located at the heart.

Physical imbalances in this energy station may result in asthma, heart disease, lung disease, issues with breasts, lymphatic systems, upper back and shoulder problems, arm and wrist pain.

Emotional imbalances here manifest as issues of the heart: over-loving to the point of suffocation, jealousy, abandonment, anger, bitterness. The big issue here is the fear of loneliness.

When this energy station is balanced you feel joy, gratitude, love and compassion; forgiveness flows freely, trust is gained.

5th energy station

This energy station is located at the throat.

Physical imbalances in this energy station may manifest as thyroid issues, sore throats, laryngitis, ear infections, ulcers, any facial problems (chin, cheek, lips, and tongue problems) neck and shoulder pain.

Emotional imbalances here may result in issues of self-expression through communication, both spoken and written. The big issue here is the fear of no power or choice and therefore feeling out of control.

When this energy station is balanced, you have free flowing of words, expression, and communication. You are honest and truthful, yet firm. You are a good listener.

6th energy station

This energy station is located in the middle of the eyebrows, in the centre of the forehead.

Physical imbalances in this energy station may result in headaches, blurred vision, sinus issues, eyestrain, seizures, hearing loss, and hormone function.

Emotional imbalances here manifest as living too much in your head, not understanding your emotions, indecisiveness, mood swings, and overthinking. The big issue here is the fear of facing your fears, and of learning from others.

When this chakra is balanced you feel clear, focused and decisive. You are open to suggestions from others and at the same time you are true to yourself.

7th Energy station

This energy station is located at the top of the head.

Physical imbalances in this energy station may manifest as depression, inability to learn, sensitivity to light, sound and environment.

Emotional imbalances here include issues with self-knowledge and greater power. Imbalances arise from rigid thoughts on religion and other rules. You are constantly confused as you struggle between what you think and what you think you should think. The big issue here is the fear of alienation.

When this energy station is balanced, you live in the present moment. You have an unshakeable trust in your inner guidance.

It is important to review your energy stations from time to time to see that they are all functioning appropriately. One sure fire way to know if your energy stations are underworking or over-working is if you start to feel stressed. Stress is an imbalance of what is going on in the collective reality and what is going on in your virtual reality. If there is too much or too little going on you get stressed. Because these energy points are located in your body you will also feel symptoms associated with a particular energy station. So pay attention to your body.

The way to give your energy stations an overhaul is to develop the skill of mindfulness. Mindfulness means paying attention. Normally when you sit down to eat a meal, you are probably talking, reading or thinking about other things. Chances are you eat in a hurry, sometimes swallowing without tasting and leaving yourself open for the conditions that go along with fast eating – indigestion, heartburn, irritable bowel syndrome and colitis, to name but a few.

Mindfulness is the skill of doing one thing at a time and concentrating on what you are doing. You savour the moment and therefore live in the moment. Start by practicing for about two minutes every day. Practice until you can practice mindfulness anytime, anyplace, anywhere for as long as you wish.

Exercise Twelve: Energy school

    ✓   For 21 days think about every food that enters your body. Keep a food diary and list all the foods you eat; morning, noon and night. Be aware of what enters your body.

✓ Eat slowly.

✓ Record when you eat the most and where. Make a note of what is going on for you to cause you to overeat. Most people overeat because of stress, boredom, loneliness, and self-hate.

✓ Try this: for 21 days eat only when you are hungry.

If you are in the habit of eating five hamburgers in a week, why not eat just one hamburger but make sure it is a gourmet one? You see, there is nothing wrong with a little of what you fancy. If you love a drink make sure it is a wonderful glass of wine. I myself love ice cream. I could eat ice cream every day. I have trained myself, however, only to eat amazing ice cream. I pride myself on being an ice cream guru. The ice cream that is in favour at the moment is so expensive and stocked by one supermarket, which is about a mile or so from my house. I can only afford to eat it once a month or so. That suits my pocket and my dress size just fine.

Choose one of the following exercises and do it.

✓ Walk 10,000 steps every day. You can achieve this by walking a little extra before work. Taking the stairs at every opportunity. Taking a file to a colleague rather than send it in the internal mail. Get creative on how you are going to achieve your 10,000 steps. You have a pedometer on your phone, no doubt, so no excuses.

✓ Dance to your favourite song every morning before breakfast.

✓ Skip rope three times a week for five minutes.

✓ Go for a long slow walk in nature. This should be at least one hour. If you can do this two or three times in the 21 days, that is great.

- ✓ Detox for 21 days. Drink lots of water to flush out the kidneys and limit your caffeine intake to two or less a day.
- ✓ Sign up for a class. It could be photography, cooking or drawing. Make sure it isn't an intellectual class, it needs to be fun.
- ✓ Invite a friend out for a drink. Spend the evening listening to them. Ask them about their job, their relationships, and their goals. Do not talk about yourself.
- ✓ Think of the people you have in your life and think about what they bring. If it is positive energy, laughter and fun, then all well and good. If you have people in your life who only get in touch with you when they want something, then perhaps it is time to move on.
- ✓ Make a bucket list of all the amazing things you would love to do. Do not censor it. If you want to swim with dolphins, so be it!
- ✓ List five things that you are passionate about.
- ✓ Learn to meditate. While you are waiting in traffic, a doctor's office or in line in the supermarket, focus on your breathing. Take a deep breath and really hold your stomach in. Hold it for a count of three and then let it out to the count of ten. Do this three times.
- ✓ Take 30 minutes' time out. Sit alone with your favourite drink and ask yourself the following questions:

"Why are you here?"

"What is the meaning of life?"

"Why am I doing this?"

"Could there be more to my life than this?"

"Is there a God?"

The only way to get answers to the big questions that you have is to ask them. Ask the questions and answer them. There are no right answers. There are only answers that work for you now. It is important that you find the answers for yourself and not someone else's idea of what the answers should be. Do your own research. Satisfy your soul!

Exercise Thirteen: De-stressing

✓ Take 20 minutes to listen to a lovely piece of music. The music should be orchestral with no singing. Go into the music. Imagine the musicians playing. Think about the mood that the music is trying to convey. Choose an instrument. Isolate that instrument from the others and focus in on it. If you get distracted, don't worry, find it again and follow. See if you can follow one instrument for a whole piece.

✓ Light a candle. Defocus narrowing your eyes until they are barely open. Look at the flame and begin to open your eyes slowly. It should take you about 30 seconds to open your eyes fully. Now close your eyes again slowly, all the time concentrating on the flame. Now focus on your breathing and take deep breath into your lungs as you open and narrow your eyes. Continue to open and narrow your eyes for about ten minutes. The first time you do this you will probably fall asleep, so make sure that you have no place to go and no one to see.

✓ Run yourself a hot bath. Fill it with essential oils of your choice. If you are suffering from stress, then lavender is particularly soothing. If you can, turn off all the lights leaving yourself a small light for health and safety purposes. Feel the water on your body. How does it feel? Think of the energy station that you particularly want to activate and place your awareness there.

"Everyone is a genius, but if you judge a fish by its ability to climb a tree, it will spend its whole life believing that it is stupid."

~Chapter Sixteen~

New Housemate: Your Self-Esteem

In order to get everything you want out of your life, it is important to have a high self-esteem. Self-esteem is your default guy. He has the spark to deal with stuff in the collective reality and the spunk to keep the housemates in line. To have and maintain high self-esteem is important, so as to move away from victim reality. In victim consciousness, your world is a battlefield, where you have to run the gauntlet between your virtual reality and the collective reality. Just think of *Hunger Games*, the movie. Everything is potentially hostile. In the victim reality, the order of the day is to blame or be blamed. You spend all of your energy not causing a fuss and keeping your head down. This is when you start to think like a victim.

"Why are they doing it to me?"

Or

"Why does this always happen to me?"

Features of the Victim consciousness:

- ✗ Blaming others or yourself when things do not go according to plan
- ✗ Not being accountable for what you do
- ✗ Having to be right all the time
- ✗ Being lazy with a 'can't be bothered' or 'it's not worth it' attitude
- ✗ Hiding in the system, thinking that if you keep your head down nothing bad will happen to you
- ✗ Gathering sympathy from others about the seemingly bad things that happens to you
- ✗ Letting an inflated ego lead the way

✘   Feeding yourself lies about your behavior. If you are good at something you play it down. If you are bad at something you tell yourself that it's because there's something wrong with you.

✘   Being stressed and alone

How would you rate your self-esteem levels on a scale of 1 - 10: 10 being amazing and 1 being not amazing?

Sometimes people talk about self-esteem and confidence as if they are the same. They aren't. Self-esteem is how you feel about yourself deep down, and confidence is what the collective reality sees based on the analysis. So if you feel good about yourself you have confidence. The opposite is true – if you feel bad about yourself, it affects your confidence.

Self-esteem is accepting yourself as you are and feeling competent and able to handle the task of life. In order to have self-esteem you need a healthy awareness and knowledge of yourself. You have to respect yourself and take yourself seriously. With self-esteem you can participate in your life rather than waiting for someone to save you. You are able to take informed risks because you know that if for some reason you don't succeed it will not destroy you, so you learn and move on. When you are successful in your goals you celebrate them and move on.

The Self-esteem housemate is loveable, respectful and has your best interest at heart. He is neutral and he goes into any situation with a blank sheet of paper, so there is no past history or hidden agenda. He listens and takes feedback well. He doesn't distort, delete or generalise information. His job is to grow and nurture you and how he does this is by logging all the great things that you have achieved. The only way your self-esteem grows is by logging your successes and achieving your goals.

No one can give you self-esteem. It isn't something you can buy and neither is it something that some people are born with and others not. You have to do the work. You have to go inside yourself if necessary and ask yourself what it is that you want out of your life. Developing self-esteem is an inside job. You need to talk to the old housemates. In fairness to them, they have taken you to this point in your life, but if they stick around any longer as they are they will hold you back. Look how far you have come in life with the self-esteem levels that you have. Imagine what you would be like if you turn up the self- esteem gauge a notch or two. What you'd be like if you went from a Level 5 self-esteem to a 9? Well, there would be no holding you back.

Exercise Fourteen: Measuring up self-esteem

Taking on self-esteem can be a bit of a challenge. Where do you start? This exercise gives you indicators about where you lack self-esteem and informs you which areas to focus on.

Health	Mental health	Finance
Spirituality	Relationships	Career

Take a look at the six categories.
Give each category a score out of 10; 1 being bad or non-existent and 10 being excellent.

Enter your self-esteem score here.

0-15 Self-esteem is an issue for you. Your self-esteem is at crisis level. You put others ahead of yourself almost all the time. You have no respect for yourself and you are willing to give away your power to others. You tell yourself that it doesn't matter and yet you know it does. It is time you took yourself seriously and placed yourself centre stage in your life. Following and repeating the 40 exercises in this book will help you a great deal.

16-30 You have low self-esteem but it is not as severe. You have your moments when you actually excel and you feel good about yourself but they are few and far between. You need to be systematic in your approach to yourself. When you have done a good job, take a moment to acknowledge your achievement rather than rushing on to the next thing. In that way your self-esteem will be nourished.

31-45 Your self-esteem is good. On the whole you have a sense of who you are, and you function well. If things don't go your way your self-esteem can take a tumble but you're able to pick yourself up and learn from situations. In order to take yourself to the next level, set yourself three goals that will challenge you. How tough they are is up to you.

46-60 You have an amazingly high self-esteem. You are your own best friend. You listen to yourself and take yourself seriously. You are self-aware and you know yourself very well, that is to say you know all the housemates and every facet of you works towards having a happy life. In order to maintain your high self- esteem, pass it on. Help someone in the community. Mentor someone at work. Give a talk at your local school. Help out at the old peoples' home down the road. Doing acts of kindness or 'paying it forward' will boost your self-esteem of the chart.

Exercise Fifteen: Affirmations

- Two minutes before you get up, tell yourself three great things you will achieve that day.
- Give three reasons why you will achieve them.
- Two minutes before you go to sleep; think of the three things you achieved that day. Think of the three special things you did to make it happen.

Exercise Sixteen: Focus on the positive.

While you are sitting or waiting for a train or in a queue, look at the others around you. Look at the person in front of you and find the positive in him or her.

Say "I love your coat." or "I love the way you do your hair." Remember to say this to yourself.

Exercise Seventeen: Give and you will receive.

When next you are at a presentation, say to the speaker that you appreciated her presentation. If someone makes a point, say to them, "You know that was a good point you made at the meeting earlier…" Notice the impact it has on them when you are positive like that. Wait and see how many people tell you how great you are the next time you do something. People will compliment you. You attract to yourself that which you already have and freely give.

Exercise Eighteen: Doing what high self-esteem does.

- ✓ Form good relationships.

- ✓ Take responsibility for your actions.

- ✓ Stop blaming and stop complaining.

- ✓ Set goals and step outside of your comfort zone.

- ✓ Get your finances in order.

- ✓ Be positive.

- ✓ The way you respond is in your power. You have the power to change your response. It's not so much what people do to you that's important; it's the way that you respond.

- ✓ Meditation: Learn to meditate as a way of tapping into your higher self. Look after your mind, body and spirit. Be kind to yourself and others.

- ✓ Value what is true for you.

- ✓ Do not take negative input personally. It's not what others say about you that is important, rather it's what you say to yourself about you.

- ✓ Beware of negative self-talk.

- ✓ Do not compare yourself to others. If you find yourself doing this, then you compare everything. Their parentage, their education; everything!

- ✓ Question yourself; do you really want high self-esteem or is there a negative pay off for staying the way you are?

- ✓ See the areas of your life that are not working as opportunities for change. You can only attract into your life those things which you feel worthy of.

- ✓ Take risks – but do your research first!

✓ View life realistically. You can't be perfect all the time.

✓ Be honest with yourself about what you are feeling, and accept the experience of your emotions without feeling compelled to act on them.

✓ Do not expect disaster. Start believing that the world is out to do you good.

✓ Learn how to accept compliments.

✓ Become aware of all aspects of your personality, the good and the bad.

✓ Discover the source of beliefs that lower your self-esteem and challenge them.

✓ Work on yourself; go to courses, classes and seminars that provide information on how to increase your self-esteem. Hang out with people with high self-esteem.

✓ Be more compassionate towards yourself.

✓ Realise that changing your self-image takes time. Once you have set it down as a clear goal you are on the way.

✓ Life is a self-fulfilling prophecy. You create it with your thoughts and feelings. What are you creating for yourself right now?

✓ Use self-improvement tapes to counter the negative inputs you may have picked up in your life.

✓ Step outside your comfort zone and challenge yourself into action. Stepping outside of our safe environment really challenges us to face our fears and beliefs. When you succeed in our goals you realise that the fears you had no longer have a hold on you and you can move on.

Act as if you have high self-esteem. 'Fake it until you make it.'

"The most beautiful thing we can experience is the mysterious. It is the source of all true art and all science. He to whom this emotion is a stranger, who can no longer pause to wonder and stand rapt in awe, is as good as dead: his eyes are closed."

~Chapter Seventeen~

New Housemate: Your Emotional Intelligence

The idea here is never to be hijacked or held to ransom by your emotions ever again. You have an IQ and it is important to develop your EQ – emotional intelligence – as well. You are an emotional being and there is no getting away from it. If you try to run away then you are not experiencing the Technicolor of life. You are dumbing down.

How can you know happiness if you do not know sadness? How can you know love if you do not know what the opposite feels like? There are good emotions and there are bad ones, but they are all there for a very good reason. When you understand the reasons you will know yourself. Your emotions talk to you every day. They give you feedback about what's going on in your collective reality. You need to know them intimately so that you can trust your instincts every time.

Your creativity will come via your emotions and not through intellect. Your passion will express itself through your emotions and not through logic. When you see true beauty it will touch your emotions and not your cortex. Can you not see what a vital side of you your emotions are?

Emotional intelligence means that you never suffer the build-up of emotions that lead to stress and ill health. You engage in open and honest communication because your mind is open and honest. People will know where they stand with you and you will form great relationships which are lasting and rewarding.

How you demonstrate emotional intelligence in the collective reality is by being assertive.

Assertiveness is the behaviour you choose when you are being your authentic self. Your authentic self has figured out what is right for you, what works for you and how you want to lead your life. No one else has the authority to do this other than you! You declare: this is me, this is what I believe in and this is what I do. I do not have to prove myself to you or get into battle with you. I am true to myself.

An assertive approach involves a genuine respect for yourself and others that you deal with.

"Thank you for calling; it has been a pleasure talking to you."

As you are increasingly able to accept yourself and all your foibles, so you become more able to accept others. You never knowingly hurt others and if you do, you do not shy away from conflict, you talk it out, openly and honestly.

"I have some concerns about what happened last week."

You do not need to put others down because you do not feel the need to win.

"Excuse me, I would like to finish what I was saying."

Instead of believing that others are responsible for your life, you can accept responsibility for your choices and behaviour. You can acknowledge your needs and ask openly and directly, even though, in doing so you risk refusal and possible rejection. If refused and rejected, you are not totally demolished because your self-esteem is anchored deeply within yourself and it is not dependent on the approval of others. You can learn to set limits assertively so that others know where they stand with you. It is from this that you get respect. You can respond sincerely to others and cope with situations appropriately in the moment. You are honest with yourself and so you are able to evaluate yourself fairly. If you 've done a good job, you tell yourself as much and if you haven't done a great job, not to worry, you tell yourself, and you figure out how you can improve.

"I think some of your criticisms of how I handled myself are valid, but I would like you to hear what I have to say and give me the chance to sort it out."

I don't want you to go away thinking that being assertive is being arrogant, far from it. Being assertive is showing balance between your virtual world and the collective reality. You do not have anything to prove. There are no hidden agendas. You do not have time to manipulate others; that is not what your life is about. Being assertive is being respectful at all times to others and equally to yourself. Your inside reflects your outside and vice versa. Being yourself allows others to relax in your company and be themselves as well.

Have a go at these exercises. They are designed for you to do in the collective reality.

Exercise Nineteen: Speaking up

1. You: When in conversations use "I" statements that are brief, clear and to the point to show your authenticity and individuality. "I" statements also mean that you are taking responsibility for what you are saying or doing:
    "I'd like"; "I prefer"; "I feel"; "I think"; "I appreciate"; "I respect"; "I understand".
2. You: When in discussions distinguish fact and opinion:
    "My experience is different".
3. You: When making suggestions do so without using the words "should" or "should not" or words to that effect. When you use words like these it makes others defensive and triggers their housemates. What you want to do is to use words that are more inclusive and which create

partnership.

"How about...?"; "Would you like to...?"

4. You: If you are being criticised, wait until you are away from the situation, so you can look at things objectively.

    Then go back and say "Do you remember Jan's dinner party last week? (*distance*) I felt irritated when you interrupted me (*taking responsibility for your feelings*). I know you have heard my funny stories a hundred times before; however, I would really appreciate it if you would let me finish in future...deal!" (d*emonstrating the right mix of empathy and coming up with a solution*).

5. You: When wanting feedback yourself, create a win-win reality:

    "How does this fit in with your ideas?"

    "I would love your opinion on my presentation."

    "How can we get round this problem?"

    "Let's look at it again."

These exercises may not come easily to you. Take them on one at a time. For example, say to yourself, "I am going to look at using 'I' statements." Practice it at every opportunity. When you have said the "I" while expressing yourself on three separate occasions, move on to the next exercise.

Exercise Twenty: Speaking out

Decide that you are going to speak up at the next team meeting. You need to say something within the first ten minutes of the meeting or your nerves will get the better of you. Once you start listening to the housemates, it will be game over.

It is a good idea when you start to speak up for yourself that you follow a structure. You will find confidence in having something to follow.

Do this brief preparation… before a meeting.

✓ Jot down a few words about what you want to say.
✓ Tell them why they should be interested or what is in it for them.
✓ Condense it into three distinct areas: tell them what you want to tell them. Tell them. And then tell them what you have told them. In other words, you should introduce your topic, talk about it and then conclude it.
✓ When you are telling people your subject matter, make sure you keep it short and to the point.

Exercise Twenty-One: Making a stand with unhelpful emotions

Think of the situations that make you feel aggressive. Write them down. Examples:

Being interrupted when you are talking/Drivers that are impolite/Bosses that do not appreciate your work. The list goes on, doesn't it?

- What is the emotion you feel?
- Where do you feel this emotion?
- Give this emotion a voice – what does it say to you?
- Give it a funny voice.
- Give the emotion a name.

I myself hate waiting in queues. It makes me annoyed. My annoyance is called 'Victor'. Actually, I have to say it wasn't me that named him, it was my husband. One day I got angry for some reason or other and he just started calling me Victor. It took the wind out of my sails completely. Anyway, back to waiting in queues. It always seems to Victor that he is behind the person who has bought items with no barcode and so he has to wait while the assistant goes into the computer to find out what it is. He also finds himself behind the person who conveniently forgot something and proceeds to hold him up while she goes in search of the item. She always has this flash of memory while she is mid-way through being checked out so it is him who has to stand there and wait for her return. The thing that really gets him the most is if she comes back with five or six items and not only the one thing that she went for in the first place. Don't try to apologise, lady!

This annoys Victor so much because he feels that people should be more respectful of each other. But I am not Victor and Victor isn't me.

So use those times when people do the things that you don't like to reflect on where the aggression or resentment is coming from.

Are these authentic feelings coming from you and only you? Or are they messages that you have picked up about how the collective reality is and how you should respond to survive?

Is it your Critical Parent saying, "If people made a list of what they needed before they went shopping, the world would be a better place"? Or is it your Ego saying, "How dare she go off and waste my previous time…what am I, the invisible woman? Blah!"? Or is it your Free Child telling you to have a tantrum or make a fuss otherwise you'll miss the cakes at the office? Is it your emotions getting the better of you and you don't know what to feel, think or say?

Use these situations that happen to you on a daily basis to go in and change or upgrade the rules.

When you find yourself getting aggressive and annoyed, keep answering the question:

"In what way does this situation happening in front of me right now affect me?"

"Is this situation that is happening in front of me right now a reflection of who I am today?"

Use those moments when things are is not going your way in the collective reality to reflect. Use each situation as a teacher. What happened? What did you do? What did you learn? What will you do differently if the situation arises again? They say that lightning doesn't strike in the same place twice. It does. Be ready!

Exercise Twenty-Two: Standing up for yourself

This skill allows you speak up and stand up for yourself in all situations where you feel criticised in any way. Learning this skill enables you to stand up for yourself without being passive or aggressive. It also teaches people in a respectful way how to treat you and defuses any situation.

Think of a situation where you felt that you were being criticised or treated unfairly. Play out what happened in your mind. Now instead of playing out the script as you know it, change the ending. Interject any one of the phrases below. Which is more appropriate? Use your own set of words.

You can:

Agree with the truth if you think that there is something in what the person is saying.
    "You're wearing that shirt again today."
    "That's right. I'm wearing this shirt."

(Here you are agreeing with the truth rather than saying, "Yeah, I didn't have anything else to wear," or "Poor me...")

This response is similar but slightly different.

Agree with the possibility or probability, however slight.
    "You're not very organised."
    "You could be right, you could be wrong."
    (Rather than: "What do you mean 'not organised'? You should talk!!")

Agree with the logic.

"If you bought a new computer now, instead of keeping this old piece of junk, you wouldn't have these high repair bills and panic every time the thing goes down."

"You're right. A new one would have those advantages."

(Rather than: "There you go again, always complaining.") In this case the other has nothing to bite on and they will soon run out of steam.

Be open to change.

"Your reports aren't presented well."

"I'm sure I could find a better way of presenting them."

(Rather than: "Yours aren't so hot either, you know.")

Use empathy.

"You're really being unfair."

"I can see how you feel that I'm unfair."

(Rather than: "Unfair? Of course I'm not unfair. It's all about you, isn't it? You're so over-sensitive.")

Exercise Twenty-Three: Standing your ground

This technique teaches you that by calm repetition – saying what you want over and over again – you can deal with aggressive or manipulative others without becoming angry or having to think of arguments. This allows you to persist with your request or point of view while ignoring manipulative traps, wind ups, argumentative baiting, or irrelevant logic.

Read these scenarios to yourself. Now write a scenario using an example from your life.

You: "I bought this pen here yesterday and it doesn't seem to be working. I would like my money back please."

Other: "Did you read the instructions?"

You: "I did read the instructions and it still doesn't seem to be working ...I would like my money back please."

Other: "Well, I have to find out who served you …we don't normally give refunds."

You: "I don't know who served me, the pen is not working, I would like my money back please."

Other: "If you have your receipt I will give you your money back."

Or

You: "I need that report by tomorrow otherwise we will not be ready for the presentation."

Other: "I cannot do it, I am overworked."

You: "I can see that you are overworked and we can talk about that at another time …I need the report by tomorrow or we will not be ready for the presentation."

Other: "Why don't you ask Radu to do it?"

You: "Because I am asking you… you are the best person to do it… I need this report by tomorrow or we will not be ready in time for the presentation."

Other: "I feel as if I am taken for granted around here."

You: "You are not taken for granted around here and certainly not by me. I need this report by tomorrow or we will not be ready in time for the presentation."

Exercise Twenty-Four: Standing up to manipulation

It is important to listen to what the manipulator says. They are going on the premise that you are a lazy thinker. They also think that you are too caught up in their charm or the moment to pay attention to the fine print. Their skill is in the ambitious and seemingly innocent nature of the words they use. On the face of it, it all seems harmless and before you know it you are being manipulated.

They say: "If I were you…I would…"
You say: "It's a good thing you're not me …"

They say: "I knew you were going to say that…"

You say: "How did you know?"

They say: "I told you so."
You say: "What did you tell me exactly?" Or "What you told me was this…"

They say: "Do us a favour…"
You say: "Let me hear what the favour is first and I'll see."

They say: "It's up to you, but…"
You say: "Thank you."

They say: "If you loved me… you would know."
You say: "In what way does reading your mind demonstrate my love?"

They say: "If you loved me, you would buy me flowers."
You say: "In what way does buying you flowers demonstrate love?"

"A person starts to live when he can live outside himself."

~Chapter Eighteen~

Your New Assistants

Now it is time to introduce you to your new assistants. They are going to be your new friends. They will not fail you.

The housemates are always chattering about something or another. It is important to have them still and silent. This frees up your energy for the things that you want to concentrate on.

Imagine if you were to wave your hand for 16 hours a day. I think your hand would get tired. It is the same for your mind. You use it 16 hours a day, every day and more, it needs a rest. To give you another example, would you leave the engine running in your car all day and all night?

If you did, you know that after about two nights the engine would lose efficiency and then stop altogether. One of the things I have heard over and over again is that it is more difficult to learn a new skill as you get older. Where that may be the case, it is not always the case. If your mind is cluttered with worn out beliefs, rules and regulations that you must check in with every time you want to do something new, it stands to reason you are not going to learn. New stuff has to get past each and every housemate.

How do you empty your mind? How do you stop thinking?

New assistant: No Mind

When you develop the skill of 'no mind', what happens is you are able to place yourself where your virtual reality and the collective reality meet. You are in no mind land. Here you get the sense of overwhelming peace and tranquillity. You have access to your creativity and you are about to bring it to the collective reality with ease.

Creativity cannot abide rules, regulations, criticisms and constraints. Creativity hates noise and particularly mindless chatter. You have to be still in mind, body and spirit before creativity comes. When you can keep your mind when all around are losing theirs, then and only then will you get your creativity.

"I just thought of something."

"I woke up with this idea in my head."

"I've got a plan, but I don't know how it will work."

"It came to me in a flash."

"I just had an 'aha' moment."

Creativity is wave energy. She comes if you are still. When an idea comes, do not, whatever you do, block or criticise it; let all ideas come no matter how crazy they may seem. The wave energy of creativity forms when and how it likes. It comes when it wants. The thing is, when she comes she needs to find an environment which vibrates at the frequency she is looking for. This frequency is open, non-judgemental, pure and free. When she finds this frequency she just keeps coming. This, my friend, is the sweet spot.

Have you noticed how many creative people say that they never read the press about themselves? Even if it is good they do not allow themselves to be contaminated with other people's ideas of who they should be and what they should do. When you are creating an environment for your creativity energy, other people's opinions will weigh you down and your idea will not take off. When you are in the zone an idea can come to you in a second that can change your world. Creativity waves do not wear watches. Creativity waves do not care who you are or where you live or how much money you have. Creativity waves do not even care if you have a PhD or a driving license. Creativity doesn't care if you are Martha or Arthur or how old you are. Build it and she will come. All she cares about is how receptive you are and how you treat her when she arrives.

Exercise Twenty-Five: Steps to no mind

- Go for a short walk
- Become aware of your feet on the ground. Talk yourself through exactly what you are doing.
- Be a narrator:

"I am walking down my road. I am going to the park for 20 minutes or so. I can feel my feet in my shoes on the ground. I am walking slowly. It feels good. My feet are relaxed. I feel the wind on my cheek. It feels good. I notice my breath is fast and heavy. I slow my breath right down and breathe from the bottom of my lungs and it feels good."

Exercise Twenty-Six: Further steps to 'no mind'

Find a quiet place to sit or lay down.

Close your eyes or defocus.

Think about nothing for 30 seconds.

It is hard to do. You may not be able to do it at first, but 30 seconds is your goal. Just keep going. You will notice that as you sit in 'no mind', even for a few seconds, you will become aware of so much more. You will hear the birds singing outside, or the air conditioning, or voices in another room. What you are doing is expanding your awareness.

Have you ever driven somewhere but you can't remember a thing about the journey? You got to where you were going safely, right? Have you ever been involved with doing something that got your attention so much that you forgot the time? Those are examples of 'no mind'.

As you progress in the exercise of no mind, you will find that you can do many things without actually thinking about them. It is as if you are on automatic pilot, but you aren't, of course. You are more focussed than you have ever been. So focussed that whatever you are doing becomes effortless.

If at any time you need to do something that needs all of your attention don't worry, you will be able to concentrate on a more profound level. Your mind will be resting but not idling and if necessary will jump to attention.

Exercise Twenty-Seven: Yet further steps to no mind

These exercises are best carried out if you go for a walk. In fact I recommend walking for at least 20 minutes every day. Call it "I" time.

Getting in touch with "I".

Walk for about 15 minutes, just allowing you to unwind from the day. Pay attention to the wind on your face. Is it a strong wind or is it a gentle kiss?

After about ten minutes of walking, begin this phrase and say this over and over again in a low voice as if you were talking to the wind.

"I am breathing."

Inhale and exhale and walk.

Exercise Twenty-Eight: Even more steps to no mind

"I am the one that breathes."

You need to practice and get to the state where when asked, "What are you thinking about?" you can answer "Nothing". Bliss!

These exercises are crazy, I know, but you will soon get used to them and furthermore, you will look forward to your 'no mind' time. What I did at first was to carry my headphones when I went walking, so that people assumed I was talking to someone or singing along to a song. Now when I do my exercises I really do not care who hears me.

I just smile and wave and do my exercises. You do the same! I guarantee you this, as you continue with these exercises over the 21 days, you will be witness to the stress falling away from you.

"If A is a success in life, then A equals x plus y plus z.
Work is x; y is play; and z is keeping your mouth shut."

New Assistant: No Opinion

What helps to keep you stuck in your mind are the endless opinions you hold about things. Having mindless opinions about anything and everything that does not concern you is one of the ways the housemates get information to keep their chat lines going. Every day the collective reality will serve you up something to have an opinion about, the housemates go to town on the opinion and finally, opinions that may or may not have anything to do with you clutter your mind. The more these opinions hang around in your mind, the more they become your reality and before you know it those opinions become your life.

You do not have to have a conversation with yourself about everything that happens in your waking hours. It is not necessary to talk to yourself all the time. You are there. You are witnessing the event. Why do you need to tell yourself that the queue is long, when you can see that the queue is long? You are standing in a long queue. Talking to yourself about how long the queue is, is a waste of mind energy, a sign of craziness and engages the housemates. Remember how it used to be?

"Oh, look at the queue."

"You should have done this yesterday."

"Now the bill will not get there in time and the credit company will be onto me."

"Why do all these people have to choose the same time as me to send their letters?"

"Oh come on, lady…"

"I wonder if the post office down the road is open."

"At this rate I won't have time for lunch."

"Why don't they put on extra staff at lunch time?"

"I have a good mind to complain."

Or

"Someone cut you up at the traffic lights."

"Stupid woman driver... it shouldn't be allowed."

"Go and race her... show her who's boss."

"She could have hit me."

"It doesn't matter …"

"Maybe I am not a very good driver and she got impatient waiting for me."

"I am getting flustered now…"

"It is important that people watch what they are doing on the road...there could have been children in the car. There could have been a dreadful accident."

"I don't think women should drive those big four wheel drives...where do they think they are, on the Serengeti?"

"Oh, I don't know what to make of it."

"I think she was drunk…"

That's how you used to be. Chattering to yourself like an old bag lady. The next time an incident occurs in the collective reality; do not say anything to yourself. Refuse to strike up a conversation with yourself. So, if it is raining, be the observer. Look at the rain. It is raining; you do not have to say anything. No comment. Now make a decision. Go out in the rain or stay home.

If someone cuts you up at the lights or jumps in front of you in a queue use this situation as an opportunity to practice no mind. I remember that a very famous supermarket built an outlet virtually at the bottom of my road. It had a restaurant, parking and many facilities for the customer. It was very convenient. One day I was travelling in the elevator to the shopping zone, when this lady piped up. From the ground floor to the 2nd floor, she proceeded to tell me that she didn't like the restaurant; the parking was too far from the shopping zone for her liking and blah blah blah. It was tempting to get into it with her. I stayed silent, only smiling sweetly. She mistook my smile for encouragement and she continued. I asked her as politely as I could if there was anything at the supermarket that she liked. It was her turn to fall silent. My words hung heavily in the air. I had put her in a double bind. If there were things she liked, why she did overlook those things to complain, and if there was nothing she liked what was she doing there? I was not going to give up my sweet spot by colluding with her. No way!

Exercise Twenty-Nine: Judge not!

As you are walking down the street or waiting in a queue, notice the person in front of you and run through this exercise.

Phase One

See the person in front of you and notice as much as you can about them. What are they wearing? What do you think about what they are wearing? If they are moving, how are they moving?

For example:

"The old guy is waiting in the queue. He is wearing a very dirty shirt. Maybe he is too old to wash it. Why doesn't he get someone to do it for him? Maybe he has no one to help him. It must be awful to be old and alone. Why doesn't he move forward in the queue? Come on, Grandpa, I haven't got all day."

Phase Two

Describe only what you can see.

For example:

"The man is walking or the man is standing in the queue… he is ahead of me."

Phase Three

Say to yourself:

"There is a man…"

So what you are doing here in this exercise is reducing the chat, the debate, opinions and the judgements about how things should or shouldn't be. When you get to the stage where you see what is, you see what is necessary to see.

When you get to this point, you will see people. You form no opinion about what they are doing or saying. It is none of your business. When you stop wasting energy by forming opinions about just about everything, you increase your mind.

Once, my good friend in Bucharest was taking me out for the day. He asked me what I wanted to do. I had no clue. I had not ventured out much in the city. We talked about the possibilities. Eventually I asked him what he would like to do. He said:

"I have no opinion. If you want to go for a walk...I am happy. If you don't want to walk, I am happier."

"Ahh," I said, trying to catch him out. "So you would prefer it if we didn't walk."

"No," he replied. "I do not have an opinion about what you do. Nor am I judging you. You must feel free to do whatever you want to do with your time, without feeling obligated."

Well, he blew my mind, literally. We went for a walk. We went here, there and wherever took our fancy, found ourselves in amazing places and spoke to amazing people. No opinion. No judgement. No preconceived ideas. Just flow and freedom.

"Never do anything against conscience even if the state demands it."

New Assistant: Listening

Listening is a key skill and an underrated one at that. You think that because you hear things that you are actually listening? Yes, you may be listening, but what about the quality of your listening? Are you listening and judging at the same time? Feigning listening just so that you can get your point across? Or are you constantly interrupting yourself and others?

Listening to yourself is key. It reminds you and others that you place yourself at the head of your universe. What you say, what you think and what you do are important. You have to hear yourself first before you can hear others. You are the measuring stick. You listen to know if what is going on is in accordance with your thoughts. You listen so that you might learn and grow. You listen so that you learn about others in your collective reality. Every single cell in your body is working flat out on your behalf day and night. Don't you think you should honour them with some respect? That is to listen to them. Get in tune with them and the way that they communicate with you. They do not have vocal cords, but they can speak.

Your stomach tells you when you are hungry. It rumbles. Your stomach tells you when you are afraid. It lurches. Your stomach tells you when you are upset. It discombobulates. Those reactions are quite different. Learn the difference, so that you do not eat because you are stressed. If you pay attention for a second your body will tell you if you should do something or not and what's more, you can rely on it. Your gut reaction to something will never be wrong. Listening to yourself and what you want to do is your sure fire way of telling yourself that you respect yourself.

In order to listen to yourself you have to start to have a dialogue with yourself. You have to ask a question and wait...the first thing that will happen is that all the housemates will jump in to answer. Do nothing, say nothing and wait...Go for a walk. Listen to music. Take a lovely bath. Go and do some exercise. Ask the question again and wait. It is then, when you are least expecting it, that the answer is there. The really spooky thing is that it will come in the most bizarre moments. There you are on the number 52 bus and you suddenly get the answer to your question. You may be watching a documentary about the most unrelated thing and suddenly the solution is there. Why does it come in such a random way? Because if it didn't you wouldn't believe it. So for example, I want to know if I should move to Australia or not. If I ask myself that question I will get 500 reasons for going and 500 reasons for not going. I ask everyone I meet. I turn the conversation around to Australia at every occasion. I become obsessed with all things Australian. Still I cannot convince myself one way or the other.

The reason why you can never believe any answer is because the answer is not and can never be factual or statistical. You can never answer a question of the heart with facts and figures. When my husband asked me to marry him, I did think about how many holiday romances end in divorce. But this was not a matter for my head, this was a matter of the soul and I said "yes". The problem you have is that you cannot wait for the heart to answer. The head jumps in with data. The head is fast, jumpy and fickle. The heart is slower and strong. And true. The heart is the one organ in your body that is never wrong! The heart is not interested in facts or figures, neither is it interested in other people's point of view. Your heart knows that in order for you to listen, it needs to be neutral and receptive.

So there you are, watching this program about snakes on the Discovery channel and the presenter proceeds to talk about snakes in Australia. He is interviewing an expert about snakes. At the end of the interview he turns to the camera and says:

"Thank you for watching…I want you to know that my years in Australia were the best years of my life. This is a beautiful country of opportunity and fun."

It is as if he is talking to you. The universe has answered the calling of your heart.

When you are listening to yourself, you are listening to your heart. It needs time to figure things out, but don't worry, the answer will come.

Have you ever had that moment when you just know something, you don't know why, but you do? These are occasions when you should always listen to your heart. If you listen to yourself, your intuition will kick in. You will actually feel an internal pull, pulling you forward and compelling you to do or say something. Everything will come together at the same time and you will instinctively know what to do. And whatever it is, it will be right!

These are the occasions that you should listen:

1) When there is something strange, different or wrong in your body.
2) When you feel that you are in physical or psychological danger.
3) If you feel that you want to help someone.
4) If you know what to do.
5) If you get the 'eureka' feeling.

Exercise Thirty: Listening to your intuitions

Before going to sleep, ask yourself a question. It could be anything…

"Is this the right person for me?"

"Should I leave my job?"

Do not think about the question, let it go…

In the morning before you get up, check to see if the answer has arrived. If it hasn't, don't worry, it is on the way.

Don't forget that the answer will not come in the format you expect. Your intuition is not on Facebook.

"I am thankful to all those who said NO to me. Because of them, I did it myself."

New Assistant: Say No

You were born with the ability to say "no". How else were you going to get a sense of who you were?

You didn't know whether you liked the blue shirt or the yellow one. You had no clue if you like spinach or carrots. How could you? By saying "no" to this and "yes" to that, you were able to distinguish your likes from your dislikes.

The ability to say "no" is one of the building blocks necessary to define who you are. As I said earlier, saying "no" does not work well in the imprint stage. It wouldn't do to have you saying "no" to the rules and regulations. That would slow down the process of your indoctrination no end. You learnt that saying 'no' and showing free will were behaviour frowned upon by the Big People. So you quickly learnt to become uncomfortable with the word.

So one of the things you are going to have to learn again is the ability to say no.

It is not aggressive to say "no." It depends how you say it. It is important to be able to say no for so many reasons. First, so that people do not mistake your kindness for weakness and therefore take advantage. Second, saying no frees up your time and energy to do the things you want to do and not the things others want you to do.

When saying no, keep your reply short and to the point. If you start to ramble, apologise or justify your no, others will see that as a lack of confidence and insist on what they want you to do. You do not have to invent excuses. This is another misuse of your energy, as you will have to remember that excuse for ever. Even though it may sound like a contradiction in terms, when saying no, keep it positive.

"No thank you, I don't want to go to the pub tonight. Please ask me next time."

Or

"No, I do not lend money to friends and family."

Or

"Normally I wouldn't mind doing the photo-copying but on this occasion the answer is 'no'."

Actually, people appreciate it when you are able to say no. It lets them know exactly where they stand with you. Of course they will be disappointed that they didn't get their way initially, but in the end they will mark you as a person of integrity. If you cannot say no then your yes is not worth much. Think about it.

Exercise Thirty-One: Telling your housemates 'no'.

Think of something that annoys you. One of my pet peeves is people with bad manners. What's yours?

Focus on what annoys you and wait. I will bet any money that one of your housemates will start talking. Let them talk for about one minute and then with a good strong voice say, "NO". Notice what happens. If they pipe up again, just say "No".

No!

Practice this exercise as much as you can when your mind starts to wander and you catch yourself thinking in a way that isn't helping you. Then just say "no" to yourself.

By doing this exercise you are training your housemates to think the thoughts you want them to think. What you want are any thoughts that positively enable you to live your life to the full. All creative possibilities, problem solving and fun loving thoughts are welcome, all others need not apply.

Exercise Thirty-Two: Saying no
- The next time someone calls your house trying to sell insurance or whatever, practice your "no." Say it three different ways and then move on to this next one.

- When you are walking in your collective reality and someone wants to stop you to sign you up to give money to charity or to sign you up to join some sect, use it as practice for saying no face to face.

Remember, all of these exercises have to be done respectfully. If you were to say no disrespectfully it is one of the housemates or their assistants talking. If you do not respect another, the object of the exercise is defeated.

*"One should not pursue goals that are easily achieved.
One must develop an instinct for what one can just barely
achieve through one's greatest efforts."*

New Assistant: Goals and Passion

In order to unleash your confidence, you need to set
achievable goals for yourself and do them. Nothing
increases confidence like the sweet smell of success.
Moving forward, onwards and upwards releases the
required energy. It is time to stop living on 'someday
island'. Someday I'll do this or someday I'll do that. The
problem with someday is that someday never arrives. Life
gets in the way. You put off your goals as if your goals are
something on the side that you may pick up and dabble
with if you get time. Well let me put you straight. You are
here to live the life of your dreams.

There is no way on this earth that you were made to
have a mundane life of repetition and chores. No way!
What are you waiting for; the perfect moment? There is
no perfect day to leave your job, go back to school, travel
the world, have a baby or switch careers. As I keep saying,
the universe doesn't work like that. It doesn't dance to
your version of perfect and neither does it keep time. You
do your thing and the universe will do its thing. When the
two of you meet, it is magic. I am always inspired by
people that go out there and do their thing.

Back to my nephew Mickey; he is never, ever at home.
He does gigs for free and he does them for beer money. He
shows up at other people's shows to watch, learn and to be
seen. He is the surfer. He doesn't know when the wave
will come but he knows that he is ready. I see people like
Mickey all the time that go out there for their art. Mickey
is a comedian. He isn't a part-time comedian. Neither is he
an amateur comedian. There is no separation between him
and his passion. He doesn't do comedy. He is comedy.
That is to say he looks at life through comedic eyes every

day. He will catch a wave. Why? Because the universe will give back to him exactly what he puts in. The same is true of you. If you put in 100% the universe will give you 100%. Imagine: 100% of the universe. All you need to do is do your passion and wait. The universe rewards commitment…always!

What is your passion? Not everyone knows what their passion is. Sometimes it is obvious. Sometimes it is under your nose and you can't see it, and sometimes you just have to dig a little deeper.

Exercise Thirty-Three: Passion probe

1) What is it that you love to do in your spare time?
2) What do you spend money on without question?
3) What did you love to do as a child but have no time for now?
4) What job would you like to try for a day?
5) If money was not a problem what work would you love to do?

Exercise Thirty-Four: Going for goals

Make a list of all the things you want in life under the following headings.

I want to	I want to be	I want to do

For example: I want to go to Japan or I want to have a nice apartment. I want to be confident or I want to be an engineer. I want to do a course.

Go through your list and make them as specific as possible. If you want to go to Japan, what do you want to do there? When is the best time to go? How much money do you need? Etc., etc., etc.

What are you willing to do to achieve your passion?

Design a mini plan around each goal. Keep it specific. Keep it small. Keep it tight.

How might you sabotage yourself?

What are you willing to give up?

In order to achieve your goals you have to give something up. You cannot have your cake and eat it too.

The main reason you do not achieve your goals is because you are not willing to give up the lifestyle that supports you not getting your goals.

Let me give you a first-hand example of this. A few years ago my friends and I started a walking club. We would step outside our front door and follow our noses. The walks were at least a couple of hours long. Some friends turned up once. Some promised to come but never showed up. Others came a few times and then became too busy. Years later I am the only one that walks. I am the founder member and now I am the only member. When I ask my friends when they complain about their lack of energy and increasing waist lines why they don't start walking with me again, they always have an excuse. They are too busy at work, it's too cold, it's raining, or it's too hot. The truth is this; they do not rate health as much as they rate ill health. They do not rate fresh air as much as they rate that fresh cake. They do not rate looking as good as they can as much as they rate the comfort and joy of the sofa. In order to find your passion and achieve your goals you have to stop supporting a lifestyle that doesn't support you.

If you want to give up smoking… you need to hang out with non-smokers.

If you want to get healthy… you need to go where the healthy people go and do what they do.

If you want to start your own business… then you need to be in business class.

You need to dissect your goal. Plan your every move. Then let it go. You let it go like the fisherman lets go of his net. He doesn't just randomly throw his net into any water. He knows where the 'sweet spot' potential is. He knows he has to be disciplined, determined and patient. He casts his net with all the confidence that his pre-planning affords him. He participates and waits; waits and participates, until he gets his fish.

It is the 'doing' that creates the tension which allows you to step into the 'sweet spot'. When you achieve your goal you positively glow. There is nothing sweeter than that! In the 'doing' you create, learn and grow. Only in the 'doing' can you experience the power of you. You become your own archetype. The person you always wanted to be like.

By achieving your goals, you step outside of your comfort zone. And who will be there to greet you? Your old housemates and their chums. But now you use them to your advantage. You become an energy shifter. You use fear as a guide rather than as a hindrance. You see anger as power, strength and fortitude. You change the 'nigglesomness' of perfection into the acceptance of your uniqueness. You use cognitive dissonance to your advantage, in-so-far as you use the tension created by cognitive dissonance to pursue what you want and not as a stick to fight and beat yourself up with. When you step out of your comfort zone and achieve your goals, no matter how small, your comfort zone grows. Your collective reality is no longer small and a dangerous place. You see that all things are possible.

"People like us, who believe in physics, know that the distinction between past, present, and future is only a stubbornly persistent illusion."

New Assistant: Living In The Moment

We live in a sound bite bumper sticker reality, where people use sound bites of the philosophy of the day. Right now, the buzz bumper sticker is "Live in the here and now." Easy to say and virtually impossible to do. As you focus on the moment, that moment is gone. At the same token, when someone tells you to live for the moment, all you can do is nod sagely as if there was an alternative. It is a paradox. It's all about balance. If you can live 80% in the present and the rest in the past or the future there isn't anything wrong with that.

The reason why you have to think about the past is because that information is vital and may get you out of trouble. It is important to ask yourself if you have come across a situation before so that you can gather as much information as you can. I agree it is craziness to live in the past, dwell on the past or to bring the past into the present. I myself thank my past; it has brought me to where I am today. I learn from the past. I have beautiful memories from the past. My wedding day. My son's graduation. My holidays. These are all happy memories that I dip into from time to time and they bring a smile to my face. Be strategic about where you spend your psychic time.

Say to yourself that you can spend time in the past only under these conditions:
- That the information is positive and uplifting
- That it is something that you have learnt
- That you want to thank or forgive the past

That's it!

You may visit the future but only under these conditions:

- That the information is positive and uplifting
- You do not travel more than six months into the future
- You convert dreams, desires or concepts into goals or forget them

That's it.

Eighty percent of your energy is spent living your life today!

You see that breath you just made, you will never have it again.

My husband and I went to see Ali Campbell, who is the ex-lead singer of the group UB40. It was an electric night. He played all the songs we know and love. My husband, as a dedicated follower of fashion, decided to film the show. Everyone was doing it. He couldn't move too much because that would distort the camera. He couldn't sing along otherwise it would ruin the sound of Ali. Days later we were relaying the show to our friends and I was surprised to see that my husband could hardly remember anything about the experience. He whipped out his mobile phone to show everyone the concert. All we could see were flashy lights and not in a good way. A moving dot in the distance that he assured everyone was Ali Campbell, and as for the sound…all it was, was a bundle of cheering and people singing along out of tune and loudly. Well, when I stopped laughing, I proceeded to tell him about the concert I had seen in 3D Technicolor, and with wall to wall sound. I had been there in the moment and I had enjoyed every moment. The concert is locked in my memory in perfect celluloid forever and I didn't need a gadget. I am the gadget!

The moral of the story is this: live your life in high definition every day. Do not reduce it to a blur on a three inch screen thingy.

Exercise Thirty-Five: Living in the moment

Choose an activity that you do every day. Let's say, brushing your teeth. Become aware of the sensation of the brush on your teeth. Focus on the sight, the sound and the smell.

Say to yourself, "I am brushing my teeth." Say it three times.

Or

Walk 10,000 steps. As you walk, focus on the ground, the placement of your feet, and the sensation of your feet on the ground.

Or

Before you get out of bed, lie there for a further two minutes and plan your day. Set the tone of how you wish the day to go.

Or

Sit and eat your breakfast or drink your coffee in silence. That means no texting, Facebook, emails, multitasking, T.V, radio, and no talking to yourself either.

Or

Imagine you won the lottery, what would you do? Let your mind wander. By letting your mind roam free without judgement, you are actually giving it a nice break. Like a vacation.

Or

While you are waiting in traffic, at a doctor's office or in line in the supermarket, focus on your breathing. Take a deep breath and really hold your stomach in. Hold it in for a count of three and then let it out to the count of ten. Do this three times.

Or

Sit in a park or your favourite place in nature. Focus on one thing, a plant or a tree. Challenge yourself to notice how many shades of colour you can see.

Or

Sign up for a yoga class.

"There are two ways to live. You can live as if nothing is a miracle or you can live as if everything is a miracle."

New Assistant: Confidence

Many people tell me in my classes that they lack confidence as if it is a virtue bestowed on only a few lucky people. That is not true. You have access to as much confidence as you want. Self-esteem and confidence are closely linked. They are more than chums I'd say, they are more like relatives. Self-esteem is the internal evaluation you place on yourself, the extent of how much you like, appreciate, know and respect yourself. Confidence is the demonstration of what you think about you to the collective reality. They work hand in hand and they are a perfect example of virtual reality and collective reality.

Self-esteem and confidence are also a perfect example of the laws of correspondence. You cannot expect to have confidence if your inner world is in turmoil. It will not happen. Self-esteem is the fuel that you need to get your confidence going. There are many people in the collective reality who think that having confidence is all about being loud and drawing attention to themselves. Far from it. Confidence is the absence of doubt and the self-belief that you can do anything you want if you put your mind to it. You have an absence of doubt because you know yourself. You have a relationship with yourself, you trust and respect yourself. Self-esteem, or the lack of it, shows the state of your virtual reality. Or to put it another way, your virtual reality is in a state. If it is a dismal and sorry place to be, it stands to reason that this is how you will view the world. Even if something happens in the collective reality, let's say at work. Someone praises you for a project you successfully completed. You feel awkward but good. By the time your housemates have finished with the praise there will be nothing left for you to take to feed your wilting self-esteem. If you have a sound, able-bodied self-esteem and someone praises you in the collective reality, your housemates know that the self-esteem must be nourished first. When this happens, the house transforms to a place of lightness and openness.

People hopelessly seek confidence in external things, thinking that they will get the prize of confidence. It doesn't work that way. As I say, it is an inside job. You have to work on your virtual reality first and foremost. You have to silence the housemates and lead them with self-esteem and your clarity in the knowledge of who you are. What you do and what is important about what you do will shine through. Once you get all of your virtual energy to flow in accord with your self-esteem, it will have no choice but to show up in the collective reality as confidence.

Your potential is particles and waves. Remember the experiment that got this book going?

Briefly, scientists believed that light was made up of particles and only particles. In the double slit experiment, scientists shone light through two slits which were then projected onto a screen. The assumption was that the light would show up on the screen as two lines, thus demonstrating that light was particles. That is not what happened; the light particles at the point of entering the slits made a decision as to which slit they would enter and as if that was not enough, they decided whether to portray themselves as particles or waves. When the scientist tried to control the light by observing it, the light remained a particle.

I could point out the analogies in this experiment, but I hope that you are actually drawing your own conclusions.

When you have got all the housemates lined up and singing to the song sheet you wrote. When you nurture, develop and guide your self-esteem. When you look at the collective reality as your place to express yourself, not prove yourself; then, and only then, will you experience the true potential of you. The things that happen to you in the collective reality do not happen because you are not a good person or someone is out to get you. The things that happen to you happen to give you feedback so that you can come back with a new and improved model. So that you can be more creative. So that you can be the one. As Pharrell Williams the singer said, "I prefer to be my number one than someone else's number two."

When you are free in your mind to make the choices that suit you given the resources available to you, then you experience the full throttle of your energy. Then you are a great particle and an amazing wave. Others will see your confidence because your confidence is an expression of what you feel about yourself.

Exercise Thirty-Six: Who has confidence?

Choose someone who in your view is confident. It could be someone you know personally or someone in the public eye.
- What is it about them that makes you think that they are confident?
- Write down a phrase that they say or would say.
- What is their style of dress?

Exercise Thirty-Seven: Confidence is an art

Read the following example:
Bill walks into a crowded room, pauses, looks around slowly and smiles. He is introduced to three people and he immediately talks to them. He uses their names. "So, Pav, what brings you to a function such as this?" He shakes Pav's hand and gives him eye contact. He listens. He dismisses himself from the group saying that he wants to get a drink. He asks everyone if they would like something from the bar.

List three positive things Bill did in your view and make it your business to achieve them the very next time you find yourself at a function.

Become a confidence beaver. Get yourself a notebook or open a file where you write up the habits of confident people.

Exercise Thirty-Eight: Confidence is a behavior

Make a list of the 20 habits of confident people.

See how many of them you can spot in a day.

And...

Choose a topic or a subject. Study this topic and become an expert on it.

A shy and retiring acquaintance of mine studied the subject of 'trees'. One day at a gathering, he asked the person next to him if he could name ten trees. The conversation spread until everyone was involved in naming as many trees as they could. My friend suddenly moved from being the dormouse in the corner to the centre of attention because of his profound knowledge of trees. He has since moved on to flowers.

Exercise Thirty-Nine: Confidence as an attitude

1) List three things you like about your physical appearance.
2) List three things you like about your personality.
3) List 30 skills you have.
   If you cannot think of 30, don't worry, just add to the list as they come to mind.

Exercise Forty: Confidence as a habit

List all the things you would you do differently if you had more confidence?

"A human being is a part of a whole, called by us _'universe'_, a part limited in time and space. He experiences himself, his thoughts and feelings as something separated from the rest... a kind of optical delusion of his consciousness. This delusion is a kind of prison for us, restricting us to our personal desires and to affection for a few persons nearest to us. Our task must be to free ourselves from this prison by widening our circle of compassion to embrace all living creatures and the whole of nature in its beauty."

~Chapter Nineteen~

Over To You

There it is...

There you have it...You've have come to the end of your 21-day Mind Synergy program.

How do you feel?

By now you should be feeling pretty amazing.

How are you going to retain this feeling?

Just as you cannot retain physical fitness, you cannot retain mental fitness. This means that you have to give your mind a workout and go through the program every so often, just to keep those housemates in their place and to update your new housemates on all the new and exciting things that are happening in your life. You need not feedback on anything other than good, positive and inspiring stuff. If things happen to you in the collective reality that are less than how you want them to be; deal with it. Make a decision. Fix it. Walk away. But never ever avoid it. Deal with things as they happen, when they happen in the moment so that they never have a chance to fester and grow. You never want to give the housemates any ammunition to cause chaos.

I would like you to take a moment to think about your energy levels at the beginning of the program and now. How do you feel?

How does it feel to be you right now? Reflect on the feelings for a moment and own them. If you do not know your feelings you will never know yourself. They are nothing to be afraid of. They are the elements that allow you to have experiences on planet Earth. Don't you think it is time that you went out and started to feel things rather than logic your way out of your own existence?

Now it's time to confront your emotions and let them know who is boss. When you marry your brain horsepower with your emotional intelligence – in other words, when your head and heart work together to support you – then, my friend, you will be formidable.

How confident do you feel right now on a scale of 1 to 10? Ten means that you feel amazing.

If you are not a 10, then what do you have to do in your life, with the people around you, with your job, to be a 10? What do you need to do to keep the 10 going?

Let's go back to the beginning of this book. Remember that I had so many problems in trying to write it? It wasn't my genre. I spent ages talking myself up, talking myself down and mostly talking myself out of writing. Eventually I stripped away all the pre-conceived notions about writing and just wrote. I wrote from my heart. It was my students that fuelled me to write. They seemed to think I had something to say. It was the stuff they sent me about energy that fired my imagination. It was only when I asked myself if I had the courage to write what I think and not what I was expected to think that the words came. It is only when I decided that I wasn't going to reference anyone else's work, or use endless examples to make my case. My story doesn't need anything other than to be told. My story is your story. Everyone has the same story. Yet it is a different story.

I went to a school reunion the other day. I was really scared. I checked myself – was it because I was looking older? Was it because there would be people there that were more successful than me?

Why had I been so nervous, apart from the ego superficial stuff, I found that the real reason for my nervousness was because I hoped that each of us had 'made it'. I hoped with all my heart that my classmates had found the key. I hoped that they could look me in the eye and say, "I am happy." I didn't want to hear any stories of doom, gloom and misspent lives. When we were sixteen, we had so much hope. We were fearless. Our favourite pastime was laughing. We thought that life was there for the taking. I hoped that they had not gotten side-tracked with stuff that, at the end of the day, amounted to a crock of nothing.

Don't get side-tracked…

When my mother died, the priest didn't say this woman was great because she accumulated tons of money. No! He said my mother was a great woman because of her laughter and song and making people happy. Her house was always open. She would take out her favourite drink that she had stashed away for such occasions. If there was food, you would get some. She would be the first to dance at any party. If there was no music she would get her guitar out and play, albeit badly. She would hold her own with strong men in a drink-off. She could have you in stitches with laughter. She was a great storyteller. She was never afraid of life.

The pursuit of money and material stuff can be a distraction.

Now, don't get me wrong. Money and possessions are important. You need to have the creature comforts of life. Why live a frugal life when you don't have to? But at the same token, why save up endless amount of money and collect stuff when you don't even know if you will wake up tomorrow? I am reminded of a friend telling me that he had escaped quite a serious car accident unscathed. The car was a write-off. He said the driver was in hysterics. "Look at my car," he kept on shouting to everyone and anyone. He had completely overlooked the fact that everyone in the car had survived unhurt.

Get your priorities right.

Of all the things we talked about, you and I, I want you to remember this.

Energy in the form of Mother Nature is beautiful whatever mood she is in. Don't you ever complain about the weather again! It shows you how out of sorts you are with the very earth on which you live. You are not the same every day. Sometimes you are happy and sometimes you are not so great. Why you expect the weather to be the same every day is beyond me. Mother Nature has bigger and better things to do than to worry about whether you can wear your shorts or not today. Get over yourself!

You are not a part of nature. You are nature.

You are not separate from nature or any other thing on this planet. You are one of them. You are a micro representation of the macro. You are nature's mini me.

You are energy in the form of a human being.

You are nature's finest and at the top of the energy tree. No other energy source, as far as I am aware, is as complicated, complex, compact and resourceful as you and your potential. When you stop to think of the hundreds of thousands of cells in your body that have to work in accordance to make you function, it is nothing short of a miracle.

Energy travels light, carrying with it only that which it needs to sustain it and those who support it. It is in the moment. That means that everything that happens now gets its full attention. It is never dispersed or diluted or distracted. The only thing energy carries from the past is the knowledge of who it is. There is nothing it needs from the past for the past is dead and the future doesn't exist. The only show in town is now.

Live in the moment.

You get so excited about a mobile or the latest gadget and the funny thing about it is that you marvel at a feature or a function that your new piece of kit can do. A feature or function that your body can do without skipping a beat. Which mobile do you know that will last 80 or so years? You will! Which gadget do you know of that renews itself every day? You do!

So my question is; how are you treating yourself?

You are particle and wave of the most complex form. You are not particle and a little wave or even particle or wave. No, you are 100 percent particle and 100 percent wave. Your particles are waves and your waves are particles. You couldn't be wave all the time as you would probably burn out. If you were particle then there would be no difference between you and a log of wood. The waves and the particle need each other and complement each other to make you who you are. If you deny any dimension, then how can you say that you are living your life to the full?

There is nothing wrong with the particle side of you. You need things to be predictable at times. You love order and security. The wave side of you craves adventure, passion, spontaneity and creativity.

In the double slit experiment, if you recall, the idea was for scientists to see how particles in light formed on a screen. To their shock and amazement, the light didn't do what was predicted. They became waves. That is to say, they did not formulate in two lines of light. Instead, they formed in wave patterns on the screen that could not be predicted. The light went wherever it decided to go. Sometimes it was wave and sometimes it was particle, sometimes it went through one slit and sometimes another. It was doing its own thing. The particles of light had a script and they were expected to do what particles of light do. It was predictable and prescribed. But light is energy before it is anything else. And so it can follow no script.

Energy is predictable in-so-far as it always flows when allowed to flow. At its core it is pure. No matter how much a lake is contaminated, when you distil it you can get pure water H_2O. Even if it is only one drop.

Energy is infinite. You can measure its density and its speed, but you will never be able to measure where it starts and where it stops.

That is the ramifications of life, right there. It is perfect because of its imperfections. It is perfect and imperfect at the same time. Like the rainbow over the slums of Rio in Brazil. It is bitter and sweet. Like sending your first born off to school. Or saying goodbye to a relationship that has run out of juice. This is the paradox of energy.

So there you have it, a single particle of light decides to be a wave. What is the difference between you and a particle of light? That tiny particle knows exactly who he is. And now, so do you.

And what about happiness? Surely I can't write nearly 200 pages and not mention the topic of happiness. You say:

"I want to be happy."

"I deserve to be happy."

You treat happiness as if it is something tangible that will visit you when you have enough or when you have done enough. It doesn't work like that. You may even think that you have to be someone special before you can deserve happiness.

"I'm a good person, why can't I be happy?"

You may be one of those who think that happiness comes when you meet that special person.

"If only I could meet someone like Brad Pitt, then all my problems would be over."

It doesn't work like that either.

What is happiness? Why is it so fickle?

Happiness has no timescales, date, size or shape issues, gender, colour, religion. Happiness doesn't care how much money you have in the bank or how old you are.

You have been told and led to believe that it is something external to you. It isn't. You been have told that you have be worthy of happiness. You have come to believe that some people are happy for some reason, yet

202

you can't fathom the reason. Maybe they are the chosen few. That also is not the case.

Let me break it down. Everything is energy. You are energy in the form of a human being, albeit a very complex one. That is what you are. Happiness is energy. You are energy and therefore you are happiness. It is fickle because you are looking for it in all the wrong places. Is happiness this? Is happiness that? Happiness is you and it has been all along. Happiness is where you are right now. Grasp it now. It is your birth right. You own it!

It is a decision that you and only you can make, when you decide to be contented with your life. Whatever is going on in your life, it is a decision that I hope that you take. I read somewhere that a baby smiles and laughs hundreds of times in a day. They are happy, not because of anything other than the fact that they are happy and happiness is them. You are happiness otherwise you could never recognise it when it happens to you. It's the law of correspondence again. If you have ever been happy in your life for one second it shows that you have the capacity for happiness. One second is all you need. You can't start a fire without a spark.

Happiness is energy and its expressions are to be found everywhere you care to look. Happiness is found in moments. It can be found in a smile, a look, a sunset, and a random act of kindness or a moment of thoughtfulness. It is found in your family. It is found in beauty. Happiness is walking in nature or dancing until dawn. It is when you laugh so hard that your sides ache. Happiness is energy doing its thing!

Your job is to have as many of those moments as you can. Cherish the moments so that at a given moment you can say:

"I am happy."

Lightning Source UK Ltd.
Milton Keynes UK
UKOW04f0103210515

251979UK00002B/5/P